Bookin' in the Big House

Bookin' in the Big House

Pat Cunningham Devoto

NewSouth Books
an imprint of
The University of Georgia Press
Athens

NSB

Published by the University of Georgia Press
Athens, Georgia 30602
www.ugapress.org

Most NewSouth/University of Georgia Press titles are
available from popular e-book vendors.

Printed digitally

EU Authorized Representative
Easy Access System Europe—Mustamäe tee 50, 10621
Tallinn, Estonia, gpsr.requests@easproject.com

Library of Congress Cataloging-in-Publication Data

Names: Devoto, Pat Cunningham author
Title: Bookin' in the big house / Pat Cunningham Devoto.
Description: Athens : NewSouth Books, an imprint of
The University of Georgia Press, [2025]
Identifiers: LCCN 2025043505 (print) | LCCN 2025043506 (ebook) | ISBN
9781588385673 paperback | ISBN 9781588385680 epub | ISBN 9781588385697 pdf
Subjects: LCSH: Devoto, Pat Cunningham | Women prisoners—
Books and reading—Alabama—Montgomery | Women prisoners—
Alabama—Montgomery—Social conditions | Book clubs (Discussion groups)
Classification: LCC HV8881 .D48 2025 (print) | LCC HV8881 (ebook) |
DDC 027.6/65—dc23/eng/20260127
LC record available at https://lccn.loc.gov/2025043505
LC ebook record available at https://lccn.loc.gov/2025043506

For my sister Sara, my partner in crime.

Contents

A Note from the Author ix

Introduction 1

CHAPTER 1
Meet Ms. Foley 3

CHAPTER 2
Conner, Our Leader 7

CHAPTER 3
Uma, the One and Only 16

CHAPTER 4
Wedding Bells 27

CHAPTER 5
Christmas Cheer 34

CHAPTER 6
Tennis, Almost, Anyone? 39

CHAPTER 7
No Parole 44

CHAPTER 8
Uma's April Fool 52

CHAPTER 9
Betty's Story 60

CHAPTER 10
Mapping Out Our World 68

CHAPTER 11
The Alabama Slammers 73

CHAPTER 12
Conner Gets "The Job" 78

CHAPTER 13
Ms. Foley Falls for Harry 86

CHAPTER 14
A New Warden . . . for Five Months 92

CHAPTER 15
Betty—Back to Tutwiler—
Again, and Again, and Again 97

CHAPTER 16
Now in Charge—Three Lieutenants and a Captain 104

CHAPTER 17
Conner Busted 110

CHAPTER 18
Linda Schools the Guards 117

CHAPTER 19
The Redneck Mafia 124

CHAPTER 20
Lessons Learned on *The Road* 132

CHAPTER 21
Our Treacherous Brownies Are Banned 137

CHAPTER 22
Our Very Own In-House Beer 147

CHAPTER 23
And Now—Banning Our Book Club Books 154

CHAPTER 24
The Final Folly 163

CHAPTER 25
We Begin Again 168

Acknowledgments 173

Partial List of Books Read 175

A Note from the Author

Years ago, when I began attending our book club, it never entered my mind that I would want to write about it someday.

Along the way, every time I took a picture or discussed other aspects of our members' prison life, I would have them sign a consent form as part of the prison regimen. They were happy to do it. Over the years I threw the forms in a stack and packed them away in a file, never thinking I would have any possible use for them. Maybe my book club gang knew better than I did all along.

This is an account of the seven-plus years I spent presiding over a book club in the Montgomery Women's Facility in Mount Meigs, Alabama.
Out of respect for book club members, and their families and friends, I have changed names and disguised identities, identifying features, and hometowns so as to protect members' privacy without damaging the integrity of the story. Many of the book club members' quotes are taken verbatim from comments they wrote down at the end of a study of a particular book.

The ongoing, confusing, and ever-present mismanagement of the U.S. prison system is an unfortunate reality.

We were not just any old book club. Twenty to life and you could qualify. Limit ten.

Bookin' in the Big House

Introduction

Driving west past the village of Tallassee on Highway 229, the rolling red clay hills of central Alabama suddenly flatten out into an entirely new landscape. Back in the day, you'd just clear off the loamy dark soil and throw in some cotton seeds and you had yourself a crop—easily accomplished with free labor, and thus perhaps the reason for the huge inequities that built up down here over the early years of statehood. It's the beginning of the Alabama Black Belt and home to the state capitol nearby in Montgomery and, incidentally, to the Montgomery Women's Facility, where I am headed. Turn right onto I-85 going south, and down the road a few more miles is the prison exit.

My monthly trek going on, what, seven years now? The time slides by and suddenly it's been seven years. Was I too stubborn to quit, or have I become like the women I'm going to see—sentenced to it?

In the beginning I knew less than nothing about the workings of our state's prison system—and really didn't care. My plan was to serve the inmates. I would go into the facility once a month, teach a class about a particular book or author, and hopefully bring some relaxation and new knowledge to the women incarcerated there.

Initially, as an author, I had been asked to give a talk to a creative writing class in Tutwiler, the state's maximum-security prison for women. (Actually, two talks, because back then the inmates with AIDS were segregated from the regular population and required a separate visit to their creative writing class.) One thing led to another and another and I ended up on the board of directors of a nonprofit to help prison inmates and realized that was not what I had intended.

Before I began writing, I had been a high school social studies teacher, and loved it. So I resigned from the board and joined Janice, another volunteer at the Montgomery Women's Facility, who had organized a book club. Several months later, Janice decided to move back out West to be near her family. Seven years later and I'm still here—with continuing contributions from my two sisters and friends and neighbors who give me magazines and books. Also, several libraries in Alabama and Georgia donate paperbacks. So while I head up the book club, it's an ongoing collective effort.

Now I divide my time between Alabama and Atlanta, although I do most of my writing in Alabama. My family's roots go back to the early 1800s, so I have great empathy for my home state. Alabama is, and will always be, so much a part of me.

In the beginning, I was fascinated by the place—by the monotony of it—by each life being lived out in the confines of a large metal building housing more than twice as many as it was originally meant to hold—bulging with bunkbeds spaced inches apart, and a constant wondering. What ominous turns in the road took them where they are, and me where I am?

In the end, wondering was useless. I was here to provide a new read each month and refreshments, along with various used books and magazines (*Garden and Gun*, old *National Geographics*, used *Southern Livings*, a few *New Yorkers*, and *People*—they love *People Magazine*) to hold the women over until our next visit and to kindle discussion of our monthly read, my favorite part, because it is very seldom just about the selected monthly read—far from it. Of course, I learn more than I teach. How conceited of me to ever think it might be otherwise.

And oh, yeah, when I first became involved with this book club, I had all sorts of pie-in-the-sky ideas. We would take our time with each book of the month. We would discuss the circumstances surrounding this author's story—that author's style of writing—the political influences of the age in which this author wrote—the plot points of each story—BS like that.

But then again, when you consider it, if you consider it, that might be ill-advised in the first place: ten women in a book club who have absolutely nothing in common, except that they have all broken the law, in varying degrees, and are all housed in the same place. Other than that, they have completely different backgrounds—big city to small town. Different cultural experiences—world travelers to those who have not reached far beyond their home county. Different educational levels—from eighth grade dropout to college degree, and yet . . .

CHAPTER 1

Meet Ms. Foley

South Alabama in mid-August. All living things bow to the sun. Grass, trees, shrubs, all shriveled up and curled into themselves—their only protection from the unremitting heat.

As I turn from the main road onto the prison grounds for my monthly visit, she is always the first one I see—Ms. Foley—off in the distance, easily visible through the high, barbed chain-link fence that surrounds this flatland compound of about five acres. She sits out in the yard beside her cart, waiting for me, ready to help unload the books, refreshments, and magazines.

Another van is parked just outside the fencing that's topped with rolls of razor wire. Day workers who have employment in Montgomery—at fast food places and beauty shops—wearing the uniforms associated with their particular job, exit the van. This is a work-release prison for women that was carved out of the larger, and more famous, men's prison, Kilby Correctional, across the road.

Truth be told, few of these women have the privilege of working in the community during the day and returning to prison each night. My book group, white shirts imprinted with "Alabama Dept. of Corrections" on the back, does not qualify for outside work release. Most of mine are in for some form of murder or manslaughter.

All female inmates in state of Alabama custody must start out and be processed at Tutwiler Women's Prison (down the road a short distance), and if they're lucky, they get sent here. This facility is, I was told upon my arrival, the country club of Alabama's women's prisons.

✳

Ms. Foley has seen my car now and stands up to pull her cart slowly toward the gate, still inside the chain-link fencing, waiting for the guard to let her out so we can unload. She looks like somebody's grandmother, wisps of gray hair held back by wire-rimmed glasses and always a smile that's kind and caring. The face is freckled from years of sun labor. She is the oldest of my ten, the only one in our group—besides me—who remembers all the way back to the Kennedy assassination.

She's been in here nineteen years so far and is in her sixties now. Once she told me that the day she shot her ex-husband, she had borrowed a 12-gauge from a neighbor—to go hunting, she had told him. She waited just outside her ex's mobile home, and when he stepped out the door with his revolver and pointed it at her and said, "I'm gonna blow your mother-fuckin' brains out," well . . .

Needless to say, her borrowed 12-gauge, at close range, took care of the rest. Of course, there's more to the story than that. There's always more to the story.

Ms. Foley is escorted to my car just outside the gate by a guard. After she and I have unloaded, everything we are about to bring in is searched. How thoroughly depends on the guard we happen to get. Some give it a cursory look and we start through the gate and have a perfectly civil conversation on the walk to the visitor center, where we have our meeting. This guard is new. He leafs through each page of each book—two boxes full of used paperbacks—then through the food, and then through the magazines. Ms. Foley and I shuffle from one foot to the other, waiting in the stifling heat.

As prisoners go, Ms. Foley is famous around these parts—for her gardening expertise. She's in charge of the beautiful flowerbeds that line the walks in the prison and the large, planted circles of flowers on the open grounds. Even in August, they still look perkier than the humans.

Ladies from one of the churches in Montgomery bring her seeds every spring, and the warden finds her a bag of fertilizer. The rest is her green thumb and lots of water and Alabama sun. Once, when the warden had visiting dignitaries, he called out Ms. Foley to compliment her on her flowers in front of them. Laughing softly, she has, in times past, told me all about her moment of grace. "All them people was impressed—if I do say so myself."

I always get the first news of the day from Ms. Foley. "Laundry room done burned down last week. Now all our washin's bein' sent over to the men's prison 'cross the road. I ain't never seen it cleaner." She winks at me as we wait for the buzzer to go off indicating the entrance gate is unlocked for the moment. "Them boys can do some good washin'." She's from the backcountry of south Alabama. Working in the soil is a part of who she is. On occasion, she gets permission to run the heavy equipment that grooms the outside grounds. And on those occasions, the others of our book club complain, "Pat, she's too old. She's gonna have a sunstroke out there."

But Ms. Foley says to me, "Rather do it myself than let somebody else mess with it. Besides, these young'uns in here now ain't got no idea how to run this here heavy machinery in the first place."

Thinking back on the day she shot him, those long years ago: "I know I done it but I'm kinda hazy in the rememberin'. Done took at least ten, maybe it was twenty, Xanax that day, tryin' to calm myself down. And some other pills too, my shrink done give me. I remember lookin' up and seein' what I thought was some kinda monster. Turned out, it was him. Said he was gonna take away my baby girl and my house and sue me to boot. And he'da done it too. He'd beat me up so many times while we was married, I wouldn'ta put nothin' past him."

While being escorted to the visitor's center, I ask the guard, What caused the fire in the laundry? He tells me—somebody smoking. After I get inside, and the guard leaves us on our own, I ask Conner, another charter member of our ten. "Does this mean y'all will have to stop smoking now?"

Conner is constantly amazed at my ignorance. "Yeah, right, Pat. When are you gonna stop listenin' to what the guards say—like they know what's goin' on in here." She hands me paper plates from one of the boxes I've brought, indicating I should start setting out ten places. "Wasn't the smoking that did it anyway. Somebody tried to clean kerosene-soaked rags in the washer and then put them in the dryer still wet, still hot. You get the picture."

"Stop smoking?" Conner looks to the others of our group, who are coming in and pulling chairs up to the table. "Is she kiddin'?" They commiserate, shaking heads and raising eyes to the ceiling. Ms. Foley touches my shoulder and smiles reassuringly.

Me: "Well, I just thought . . . if smoking causes . . ."

Conner: "Yeah, right, Pat. Pass me some of those cups . . . please."

Of course, upon consideration, they're right, as usual. Most of my ten have been here ten to twenty years longer than any of the guards. Guards and wardens come and go. My ten are the bedrock.

It was the first thing I learned here, many years ago. There are at least two stories for every happening in here. You choose which one to go with, like sweet Ms. Foley's story. Some of my ten have told me that they heard she's in here because she helped hide her husband's body after her son killed him and that her other children had helped too. Now they are all serving time in different Alabama prisons. Not a likely story, but an interesting one, told a while back and passed on to me as my ten sat in the evening shade of the huge metal building they call home.

Ms. Foley's story has never wavered. She killed him herself because he abused her and her children for years, so she shot him. In the telling, she says that her gun only held one shot and her husband's pistol held six, but "I got 'im 'fore he had time to get off a round." She explained this to me one day as we looked out over her lovely, brightly colored flowers growing in the beds that dotted the grounds.

All I could think to say was, "Well, Ms. Foley, you saved your children from years of abuse." She nodded, seeming completely satisfied with her deed. Through the years, whenever our group talk turned to life stories and how they ended up in here, most would equivocate—"I woulda done it this way if I'da had my mind about me." Or "I really shoulda not been drinkin' that night."

Ms. Foley always said the same: "I done what I done."

CHAPTER 2

Conner, Our Leader

Finally, as we had finished with the preliminaries of checking in, and unloading all our goodies in the room where we meet, other members who had come in couldn't hold back telling me—so pleased were they with the read this time. "Sorry, Pat, but we read the whole thing—the whole of the *Poisonwood Bible* book."

Ms. Foley, grinning, said, "You knew we would."

I feign disgust but am secretly delighted that I've found one they like that much. I had thought they might relate to this story of a born-again preacher who took his family to the wilds of Africa on a mission to save the Natives. But it's a long story, and I was afraid it would look imposing when I first handed it to them.

"But I told y'all, don't—do not—read the whole thing this time around."

"Really, Pat, you knew we would." Conner pitches me some paper napkins to arrange next to the paper plates. Conner is in her early fifties and has been here since she was in her early thirties. Somehow, we all feel Conner should be telling us what to do—short-cropped graying hair, she's got things under control—and you better believe it. Her full first name is Constance but the nickname, Conner, is more of who she is in here. Upon coming into a room, she immediately presents as solid, mentally and physically, ready to defend whatever and whomever might cross her or any of her group. "Gay for the Stay" probably fits her lifestyle for now, as it does so many in here. To come into this place, thrown aside by the real world, there must be a great longing to connect with another human being.

I dutifully begin placing napkins. "Y'all know our book of the month was a blockbuster when it first came out. It probably sold a gazillion copies."

To give them an idea of Africa's size, last month when I had given them the book to read, I had passed out maps of the continent and superimposed on it, all the other countries that would fit into its boundaries—the United States, India, Japan, et cetera. I thought it was fascinating. They weren't impressed.

I had assigned the first half, thinking they would read that and not be overwhelmed with the whole book. My plan—silly me—was that we would talk about plot, characters, the far-reaching implications of the Congo's fight for independence from Belgium, and then they would read the rest of the book for next month's assignment.

Harriettee (that's the way she spells it—says it gives her a more cosmopolitan flavor) smiles condescendingly at me and says, "You should have known, when we found out at the first of the story, that the mother had left one of her children in Africa. We had to read on, to see what happened to the kid."

As usual, my carefully arranged agenda was out the window.

As a group, they loved the story, especially Harriettee—tall and thin, she's a former high school mathematics teacher from up East—world traveled—sunny and sarcastic. She will, she declares with a wink—if she ever gets out of here—go to Africa and open up a bar in South Africa, like one of the characters in the story.

Perfect, I think to myself, since Harriettee is in for being a big-time drug abuser. "I had my first child by cesarean and was on strong medication for that. I went straight from the hospital to the street looking for those same drugs." Her third husband, or was it the fourth, was a dealer. Says she married him for the convenience of it. Just got hooked and couldn't get off.

I had been informed early on by my book club members that you can get drugs in here anytime you want them. Work release is like a sieve, filtering out very little, but Harriettee is steering clear for now. She's an exception in our book club—not in for some degree of murder or manslaughter. I was told when I came into the book club that the rule was twenty to life—murder or manslaughter—and you could qualify to join our group. Somehow Harriettee is a member. Again, two stories.

I reiterated to all of them last month when I gave them Poisonwood Bible. "Only the first half—read only the first half. It's long and y'all have other work to do." At the time Harriettee was getting up at 2 a.m. to work in the kitchen. Breakfast is served at 4:30 a.m. "Don't," I said, "under any circumstances, try to read the whole thing. We'll take our time with this one. It's so good."

What did I think—they were going to follow my instructions to the letter of the law? They're all in here for breaking it . . . really, Pat.

Food always comes first: Subways, chips, Cokes, and brownies my sister had made, without nuts, since one of my ten—Harriettee—is allergic to them. Paper plates with the University of Alabama logo on them. Big football fans in here, and this is the beginning of the season. Next time I will need to bring Auburn University paper plates. Of the two TVs in this facility, one is dedicated to sports alone. I am told that there is a long-timer who is a fanatic about sports, of any kind, and somehow she has corralled the channel changer and won't let go of it.

We talk and eat and, as usual, about halfway through our book discussion, all—all except Val—get up and walk out for a smoke—roll-your-own. Here you can buy the makings in the prison canteen—cheaper that way, and I imagine a lot more variety as to what you can roll into your own. When the craving calls, one gets up and then, en masse, they all get up and walk outside the visitor center door and stand on the concrete sidewalk that has a No Smoking sign painted on it—and they smoke.

I reason it's not for a lack of manners that they get up right in the middle of whatever I, or one of them, might be saying. It's just the lifestyle as dictated by the circumstances. Conversely, good manners manifest themselves in other ways. During the talk, eat, discuss portion of this visit, I needed to avail myself of the facilities. All, unanimously, reached into pockets and offered up a portion of their monthly ration of toilet paper. Prison etiquette.

Val, my only nonsmoker, stays behind to catalog the books I bring in. She's been in so long, she knows all the ropes—works, sometimes, in the administration office. You want to know something, you ask Val—very organized. The long chestnut hair is pulled back in a very practical ponytail. In her former life, she was an accountant. When the others go out on smoke break, she gets up and immediately starts going through the extra books and begins to list them all on a yellow pad. She marks each spine MWF. It seems that, if they aren't marked, some of the short-timers try to sneak out with books when they get parole or it's EOS (end of sentence) for them.

The next month Val will bring me an updated typed list so we have a running tab of everything that has been brought in—and, incidentally, she has first choice as to what books and magazines she wants. She obviously has the ability, one the others don't have, to get something typed up and printed out in here.

As the others are still out smoking, she tells me her story. Val is rather stocky now, with a ready smile, and brown eyes that look out of black framed glasses, but she says when she was thirteen years old, she weighed in at 240 pounds. Her parents approved bypass surgery for her when she was fourteen. She was born in North Dakota, has lived in New Jersey and Arkansas, and now here she is in an Alabama jail. In for vehicular homicide.

"My mother wasn't feeling well, so I got in the car to go see about her and I had been drinking. I'll admit that. I tried to pass a car when another one was coming in the opposite direction. The person in the oncoming car that I ran off the road was with her aunt who was visiting from up north. . . . Auntie was killed."

She's been in for fifteen years, so far. She pitches another paperback into the pile of initialed books and looks down at the remaining unmarked stack. "The Lord didn't want me to have those five extra seconds it would have taken to get around that car."

Now all are back in the room after smoking break—and the discussion continues. It was not long after I started coming to book club that I realized the books themselves were just incidental to the gathering. Perhaps that is the way with most book clubs. We hold up the book and say we have read it—whether we have or not—and it becomes our ticket into the group. The book itself simply serves as a backboard, and we bounce our lives off its contents. And one thing for sure, this group has plenty of bouncing to do.

Most were disgusted with the father in Poisonwood Bible, a born-again preacher who constantly bullied the family through his biblical interpretations.

Conner, whose mother made her marry her abusive boyfriend because she was pregnant, said the mother in the story was just as much to blame for letting him get away with it. "Mothers are supposed to protect you, for God's sake—not send you down the rabbit hole to hell."

Ms. Foley said the preacher man was to blame for it all and she couldn't understand it. "A preacher? A man of God? I always loved my preacher. Don't understand this here one. Why was he draggin' them children all over creation—way out to Africa?"

Harriettee was still enthralled by the sister in the story who ended up running a bar in South Africa. As an army brat, she has lived in other countries and knows the lure of foreign climes. "I can see me now, cigarette holder in hand, sexy low-cut blouse on, and I'm greeting customers. That's me to a T, baby."

While the rest of the group seemed to give the book an A rating, Val said it was slow in places. The accountant mentality in Val never seems to give any read a perfect score . . . or she didn't read the book in the first place.

After a few more minutes of discussion, the conversation wanders, as it always does. They either can't or won't stay on any one subject for more than a few minutes at a time. Is it years of early childhood trauma, or years of illegal drug use? Or maybe I'm boring. Who knows? It is as it is.

The talk turns to a lawsuit being brought against Tutwiler, the big women's facility through which everyone must pass when first coming into the Alabama state prison system. Even now my girls occasionally travel back there for dental checkups and other appointments. As a consequence, there is an open pipeline of communication between the two facilities. Not to mention those who get sent back to Tutwiler from time to time for major drug infractions and then, hopefully, return to us.

It seems Tutwiler is ripe with transgressions. Conner says, "It's rape anytime a guard has sex with a prisoner, consensual or not, Pat."

It hadn't crossed my mind, but of course it had theirs. Some said they knew of girls who got pregnant and then disappeared from the system—paroled or let go early, to get rid of them. The guard involved gets fired and that's the end of that. Recently these contraventions have been made public and now the press is . . . pressing, and so is the public, and finally the public officials.

Now Harriettee gets up to leave, saying she can't stay any longer because she has to earn some money by rolling cigarettes and ironing.

In here, you can have an account to draw on—to buy stuff at the canteen (sandwiches, candy, chips, extra toilet paper, cigarettes—regular or roll-your-own)—if you have someone to send money to it. Otherwise, you have to find ways to earn it on your own.

No-nonsense Conner says she earns extra cash by handwashing other prisoners' clothes and ironing them. And in response to my quizzical look, she says, "Yeah, Pat, we all have our hustle in here—it's illegal of course, but ya gotta do whatcha gotta do." A shrug of her shoulders.

All too soon, it is time for them to select from the extras—used paperbacks and old magazines I bring. A stampede to the two big cardboard boxes I've brought in and Val has inventoried.

Ms. Foley loves anything by Debbie Macomber. Val likes Nora Roberts, Harriettee favors Philippa Gregory. She is now stashing her finds in the back waistband of her uniform so she can hide her books by pulling her shirttail out over them. "If I take them back to the dorm in hand, everyone will rush up and want to borrow them and I'll never see them again. This way I can get them back to my box before they notice." She looks at me with a condescending smile, "Yes, Pat. I'll share—when I'm finished."

The time is up. Everyone scurries out with their respective hauls. Linda steps forward. She's in charge of the library. She takes what remains of the books and magazines to be stacked in three small bookcases—the prison library, such as it is. She has to keep winnowing out the books to make room in the limited space. Nearly every other square inch of their living space is filled with bunkbeds: the main dorm room, out in the halls, by the indoor rec area, anywhere there is open space.

From time to time, well-meaning souls will donate stacks of used books that they want to get rid of, with subject matter that no one in here would be caught dead reading—the thought being, I suppose, that "in prison anything to read is better than nothing at all to read." And after a short grace period, those books are summarily pitched.

Librarian Linda has been in for over twenty-three years, and although she is not a librarian by trade, she is in here—very organized and efficient. Also, she serves as our unofficial book club secretary. If ever I have a change of plans at the last minute and can't make the monthly book club date I've promised, I write to Linda to reschedule and she passes it on to the others. She, and the others, write back from time to time with tidbits of what's going on in their world.

You never see Linda without being reminded of her former life. One arm is slightly shorter than the other and not able to bend much at the elbow. Seems that in her other life, her boyfriend beat her up so badly that, although she has had surgery twice to try and correct it, there is still ample evidence. In addition, but not as noticeable, is dental work that is needed to correct missing side teeth, evident when she smiles. One can only imagine what went on to acquire that look.

As I pack up to leave, I chat with the girls and hear the latest rumors. This one is about hoped-for prison reform. Alabama has long had one of the most crowded prison systems in the nation. As a first step toward improving the prisons, the Alabama legislature is again considering prison reform legislation—as it does almost every year. (No one ever seems to consider serious reforming of the sentencing laws that are sending people here to be literally stacked on top of one another.)

Among my ten, there is much discussion about how this might affect the long-timers like themselves. Maybe they will be able to qualify for outside work release—maybe they will come up for parole sooner than expected—or maybe, just maybe, they will be let out, just let out and told to go home to relieve the overcrowding.

There are also rumors that Ms. Foley might be up for parole soon. Or that Harriettee might qualify for work release, or that Val and Conner will get let out one of these days. Rumors float around here like lighting bugs on a summer night—constantly grabbed for or swatted at, upended and altered to the point of becoming entirely new stories.

Another of our book club members, who has been in for many years, was recently turned down for parole—again. She wonders, out loud, if she should talk to her lawyer and have him do something, or should she get another lawyer? The others stare into space, waiting for her to finish talking, knowing that she doesn't now, and didn't ever, have a lawyer, but it does sound good and it seems to make her feel better. She hums a little tune as she leaves with her books.

I suppose if you sit on your bed for years at a time, looking out through the maze of bunkbeds surrounding you, breathing in the steamy hot air that is south Alabama in the summertime, swatting away the flies that come in through the doors and exhaust fan vents, pipedreams begin to morph into your wished-for world.

I mentioned in our last meeting that I would like to see how their living space is configured, as they were constantly complaining of the crowded conditions. I received a drawing in the next letter I got from Linda—compliments of Uma, one of our members. I count 145 bunkbeds—290 sleeping accommodations in this particular configuration. Extra beds in the day room and along the wall in the main dorm. No AC, of course.

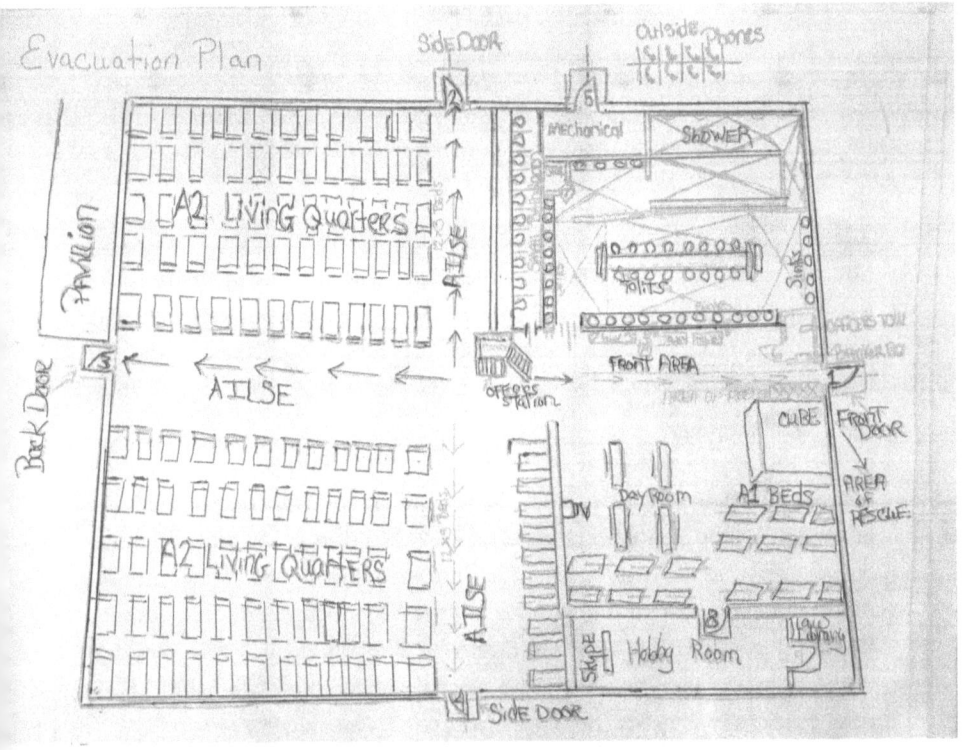

An evacuation plan for the Montgomery Women's Facility

CHAPTER 3

Uma, the One and Only

The weather is blessedly turning cooler, certainly not cold but not blazing hot, which will give some relief to the scores who inhabit the giant dorm room and every other nook and cranny that can hold a bunkbed. The big exhaust fans give a cooler breeze now. The flies, which have numerous entrances from the outside, are not so bad as to keep the inmates from sleeping at night.

On the way in this month, Ms. Foley is discussing, with the escorting guard, an inmate who just came into the prison and is hitting on her. The girl, who is young enough to be Ms. Foley's child, is going around prison telling everyone that Ms. Foley is her honey—much to Ms. Foley's amusement. "I ain't foolin' round with no honeys." Ms. Foley is of the Southern Baptist persuasion. Honeys and Southern Baptists do not mix. Besides, both the guard and Ms. Foley agree that this new one is probably "'bout three bricks shy. Place is full of burned brains," she tells me.

Someday I must pose this question for discussion in one of our meetings: Is prison the ultimate in diversity, or what? You've got your white, your Black, your Hispanic, your old, young, gay, straight, trans, crazies, and you might even have a few innocents all squeezed in together sleeping inches apart, and yet they all must get along because, of course, if you step out of line, there is a larger dictatorial force to be reckoned with. Fights do break out from time to time. I check in some months and immediately find out that there was a big fight between two inmates that the guards had to break up, and in the process the guards sustained welts and bruises, as did the two women inmates who were mixing it up.

My ten look with much disdain upon most of their fellow bunkmates, especially those who are in for short-term sentences. Seems the "short-timers" are considered lowlifes in that they don't know the ropes, can't be counted on to share the workload, don't care to do anything but sit around watching TV and use the prison as a revolving door. And if they become

disgruntled, they might stuff a few Kotex pads down the toilets and over-
flow the whole sewage system—messing up the house my ten call home.

Ms. Foley, in an aside to me, as we walk across the yard: "Old Jamie
Lou over there—back again. Stayed out all of nine months this time. Got
the same bunk she done had last time she was in here. Just kinda wanders
in and out, in her own world."

People assume that my book club will be mostly Black and that most
inmates in here are Black, given our location in the Alabama Black Belt
(which in fact takes its name from the color of the soil, if you are ignorant
of Southern nomenclature). Actually, just over 50 percent of the women in
here right now are white. Most all of the guards are Black women. Sometimes I hear stories of discrimination against whites—but not concerning
my ten. They seem very compatible and caring of each other—in my presence anyway. Of course, that would be helped along by the fact that my
ten generally choose who will take the vacant place if someone is paroled,
sent back to Tutwiler, sent up to Birmingham (one of the other women's
facilities in the state), or escapes. I later found out that one of my ten had
tried it—escaping—for a short time, years ago.

In times past, they have humored me by pretending it's a democratic
process as to who is asked to be in our book club. "Okay," Conner said,
looking to the others and smiling, "I nominate Uma [or whomever] to
take the empty spot. All those in favor raise your hand." All the hands go
up. "Aren't you gonna vote, Pat?"

I raised my hand—like I had a say in the matter to begin with—and
smiled as I nodded to Conner: "Such a pleasure to be included." She
pointedly ignored the sarcasm, made a quick face at me, and continued.

The fact of the matter is that I would rather not have a say, as they are all
strangers to me, and she knows it. Although I do check their incarceration
records online, Conner also knows that there are those who are illiterate
and would not care to be asked in the first place, and if they were, they
might join and pretend to read the book—for the refreshments alone.

On to the book of the month. *Mao's Last Dancer* was a hit—for those who read it. I can usually tell who has read the monthly novel and who has pretended to. Harriettee, Ms. Foley, Conner, Linda (the librarian, of course), and Betty (when she's not high on one drug or another) are ardent readers, but I don't kid myself—the expanded refreshments I've brought, as recently okayed by the warden, might be the main attraction. I think, at times, that one or two of them have been given a crash course on the novel of the month by one of the other ten, right before they come into book club. I'm not happy with this method, but hey, there are myriad ways of learning.

Our book of the month sold like wildfire when it first came out—and it's a true story. Where possible, I like to read nonfiction.

You will notice, as we go along, that we read with no particular theme in mind. Basically, we read what I can find ten copies of—secondhand and in paperback. If they have been off the best-seller list for a while, I can usually get a bargain. From time to time, my donating libraries have asked me, "Why paperback? I have some great books in hardback that you would be welcome to." My reply is that I have heard several theories: that possible weapons could be made out of the hardback's cover, that paperbacks are more easily stored. The real reason doesn't matter to me. The rule is the rule. I do as I am told. Why rock the boat? It gets rocked enough in here as it is.

✳

Conner is not happy with the main character in our read—*Mao's Last Dancer*. It's about a young Chinese boy who joins Madame Mao's Beijing Dance Academy, becomes famous, and eventually defects to the United States.

"It took him long enough to figure things out, for heaven's sake—half the book." Conner doesn't have much empathy for people who struggle outside the gates of Montgomery Women's Facility. "If I'da been in his shoes, I'da left China ages ago."

"Like you gonna just up and leave China," Uma says.

Harriettee, our much-traveled army brat, was fascinated by China and how the society was dirt poor and yet gave this unconditional love and loyalty to the *Dear Leader*, and then how the main character finally began to have his eyes opened and discover a way out. "On a scale of 1 to 10, I give it an 8."

Ms. Foley: "He was poorer than me when I was a young'un and that's hard to be."

Uma: "Does everybody wanna come to America? All I ever be hearin' is peoples be wantin' to come to America."

Uma, arrested years ago, was the first member we asked into our book club when there was an opening in the original ten. When she talks everybody listens. Whether it's true or not is beside the point. Always a smile that shows off her gold front tooth and a funny story so subtle it takes a second to catch on, and then everyone is laughing. Uma was arrested in south Alabama, where her mother's family has lived for generations. She says her kin were on the boat that brought the last slaves to America, back in the mid-1800s, when the *Clotilda* docked in Mobile Bay and brought in more than one hundred enslaved people from Ouidah, a city on the west coast of Africa. They eventually established Africatown, just north of Mobile. There is a sense of self in Uma that would have to be a product of generations of proud people who know their history, and are happy to tell you about it. "My family, they helped to set up the Hopewell Baptist Church in Plateau. That's what Africatown used to be called, Plateau. Why, when I was little, we had to go to church every Sunday. On Sunday morning my daddy, he would be up drinkin' coffee and playin' church music on the radio, and he'd been flat-out drunk the night before. He'd shoo us all off to church. When my kids come along, I done the same thing with 'em."

Uma smiles, as she is the center of attention now. "Peoples say I look a lot like my mama. She has yellow skin and red hair, what Black people call Redbone."

"My daddy, he sold pills but his main job was fraud—went to federal prison twice for it. My momma, she sold her own pills."

Uma continues to reminisce. Said the gun she pulled out that afternoon, long years ago, was just to scare the girl she'd been arguing with. Said she didn't even know the bullet done gone through the door and killed somebody.

I believe she originally had a twenty/five split—meaning she would have been up for parole in five years—but Uma isn't one to shy away from confrontations, and they do come, regularly.

She told us she was talking to her son—who's being raised now by her mother—not long ago and he said he remembered the day of the shooting, when he was a young child. He's an adult now. In addition, she says she has a daughter who has recently been awarded a four-year scholarship to one of the Alabama universities and will be starting soon.

She smiles across the table to the rest of us. "I was talkin' to my favorite aunt a while back. Told me my dreams are waitin' for me to fulfill 'em. This is just a restin' period—I still got the power to do anything in life."

In prior sessions, I passed out individual maps of the world for them to keep under their bunk. (Everybody has a box, kept underneath their bunk, and searchable.) We place a sticky circular tab on the country in which our monthly book is set. Maybe get an idea about the geography of it all. So this time they plunked one down in the middle of China. Once when we were reading a novel set in France, one of the girls started to place her sticker in South America. Some others placed stickers in equally varied places, but as a whole, this is a bright group. The range of formal schooling for my ten is quite varied—repeat, *formal.* Ms. Foley dropped out in eighth grade. Harriettee has a college degree. Others dropped out in the tenth or eleventh grade—some pregnant.

The discussion of *Mao's Last Dancer* didn't last long. It quickly evolved into talk of another inmate's wedding.

You are saying to yourself, Why didn't she just steer the conversation back to *Mao's Last Dancer?* Because—hello—who wouldn't want to find out about Rosalee's wedding plans? She's getting married—in here—in another few weeks, and because she's one of us, my ten are in charge of decorations, food, photography, all the trimmings. The name is a perfect fit. Rosalee reminds me of a flower—delicate and evidently easily bruised. I was told by the others that somewhere along the trail of her incarceration history, she had become very depressed, but a new day dawned when Rosalee met this fellow, who was originally from somewhere in Great Britain.

They started corresponding, he moved to the United States and began visiting her . . . and they fell in love.

Right now, he has employment as an IT guy down on the Mississippi coast. They talk almost every day on Skype—a service recently introduced to this prison. Now they are getting married, even though it will be in name only. You are not allowed conjugal visits in here. He's working hard, he says, to get her a new trial and out of jail. She is thrilled and excited. The others are thrilled and excited to provide the wedding trappings.

Am I a cynic to think the groom might have an ulterior motive? I suppose I am, but then again, love is love—no matter where you find it.

And another big event of this visit—Sara is here for the first time. My sister had wanted to come for a visit on several occasions but she has health issues and has to accommodate them. From the beginning of book club, she has helped me gather books from local libraries where she and her husband live in the North Georgia mountains. In addition to the books she has, on occasion, sent them a special hand lotion she makes that is completely free of anything but natural, environmentally friendly ingredients. If I am a middle-class law-abiding geek, my sister Sara is a middle-class environmentalist geek.

When we had checked in on this visit, Ms. Foley greeted us at the gate to help with books and other paraphernalia. Sara shook hands with her and Ms. Foley immediately gave Sara a big hug and called back across the compound to the other girls. "Sara's here, Sara's here." In return, Sara, having heard all about them, had tried to memorize their names beforehand and they loved it—so impressed and pleased that she had gone to that trouble.

It didn't occur to me at the time, but I suppose interacting with a new face, a new personality, unlike what they would meet in the bunkbed maze, is a big deal. Sara is the antithesis of everything in the bunkbeds—with a model's figure, she's retired now but has had a long career in marketing and advertising. She meets and greets with a warm smile and an earnest handshake.

It also happens that Sara, among her other many talents, is an award-winning photographer, so she and Conner immediately began comparing notes. Conner will be in charge of Rosalee's wedding pictures and wants some advice. She has been in jail for more than sixteen years at this point and so is probably not up to date as far as the latest photographic techniques. Her intense blue eyes take in Sara's every suggestion. All the while Sara is interested in Conner and her life story. So, between talk of wedding photography, Sara is asking a question here and there about what brought Conner to the Montgomery Women's Facility.

Everyone, of course, has a story about their life prior to prison time, and this is Conner's, as told to Sara, as they chatted quietly together in the corner during refreshment time. Conner was in the wrong place at the wrong time—with her boyfriend in a drug house when the police raided it. Her boyfriend killed one of the cops. Conner believes that because she was in the state of Alabama when it happened, as an accomplice she got the same sentence as the shooter. I haven't ever tried to dissuade her notion that Alabama is unique in that respect. What good would it do—and what difference would it make now?

All the while, Librarian Linda is making the wedding decorations for the walls—crepe paper, balloons, and such. Others are planning centerpieces for the tables. Rosalee is allowed to have a few guests, so I suppose it will be mostly family, along with most of the book club gang. The wedding will be in the visitation room, where we meet every month. It's a space large enough for eight to ten vinyl-topped tables that can seat four people each. Also, it has two AC window units, which come in handy when the temperature soars. The ceremony will take place in among the vending machines used at visitation time, amid stacks of Bibles on one of the tables for Bible study class, and the bulletin boards that line the walls. To one side, there's an upright piano, I suppose for church services, and maybe it will be used during the upcoming wedding celebration.

It seems Rosalee was high at the time she was supposed to have killed a man. She says she doesn't remember. Aside from her obviously delicate nature, Rosalee is tall and thin with long blond hair. Her makeup is always meticulous—perfectly outlined lips in bright red, a slight blush to the cheeks—the antithesis of Ms. Foley, coming in out of the blistering sun just having cut a swath of grass in hundred-degree weather. Rosalee always gives me a hug when she comes into the room. Soft-voiced and self-effacing, sometimes barely heard above the din of book club talk. Twelve years so far.

Right after our smoking break, while everyone is being reseated and we are waiting on the stragglers to come back in, I ask about one of our ten who is absent this time—a new girl who looked to be still in her teens. I had seen her very briefly last meeting, but now I am told that she's been shipped back to Tutwiler. Nobody wants to go back to Tutwiler. I remember her as very pretty with short brown hair—in for murder. Bad things can happen at Tutwiler.

At present, there seems to be a constant shifting of inmates to and from other facilities. I learned fast that this shifting of prisoners is endless. I will come in one month and everyone will be here. The next month, some have gone, or have been sent, back to Tutwiler for various infractions. Others have left and gone up to Birmingham Community Work Release or the Tutwiler Annex. This time, in addition to a young teenager, some others of our ten had been shipped to Tutwiler last month. It's an ongoing rumor that this facility is going to close down and everybody will get placed in other facilities. But then again, I think it has been an ongoing rumor for several years now.

"Maybe," Conner says, "they'll send us to Louisiana again."

"Louisiana? Why Louisiana?" Once again, my inexperience is showing.

Conner takes a long sip of Coke and sighs. "Okay, Pat, it was this way. All of us were sent to Louisiana a few years back." She turned to the others for backup. They nodded.

"Private prison," Linda says, "till Alabama ran out of money or wouldn't pay the bill, or something like that. Then we got sent back here."

"True," Conner nods. "Every time there's overcrowding and the Feds show up to do some countin' we get shuffled around to make the numbers look right."

"Yeah," Linda says. "You get sent someplace for three days and then sent back. Never know where you'll end up. Louisiana was different. We were there for a year or so, as I recall. Shuffled us over there for a while to get the numbers looking better over here, I guess."

"So you ended up back here at a work-release facility and not really on work release."

"We were the lucky ones," Val says as she places the last of the marked paperbacks in a pile and begins to stack them. "Louisiana Leftovers, we were."

Thinking that this would have been a terrible experience—knowing the reputation of Louisiana prisons, I couldn't help but ask.

Conner: "Oh, no, it wasn't bad at all." The others nodded in agreement.

Ms. Foley: "We had stuff to do all the time over there—goin' to classes and such. Done got my drug-free certificate over there—still got the paper. We don't have nothin' to do here."

"Well, you have classes you can take here."

They think that's funny, looking at each other and then to the ceiling.

Conner: "Really, Pat, we've taken every course offered at least fifty times over. Dave Ramsey's video course on financial planning—we know that one by heart."

Linda: "You wanna know what I do all day?" Without waiting for my reply, she begins to recite.

> Okay—6:00 a.m., wake up—brush teeth, get dressed—all that. Yeah, I know breakfast is at 4:30 a.m., but who can get up at that hour.
>
> 07:00—I go to my state job—taking care of the library, to get it in order—which takes about as much time as you would expect with so few bookcases. Then go outside to get some fresh air.
>
> 9:00 is the count, and then I go outside to get some more fresh air.
>
> 9:00–4:00 p.m. I bathe, crochet, write letters or read, make cards to send out, teach crochet, cook, go outside and get fresh air again, roll cigarettes.
>
> 4:00—I check on the library again to straighten the books. After that I read, roll more cigarettes, go outside to get more fresh air, and go to whatever extra-curricular activities might be offered.
>
> By 10:00 I am in bed reading and asleep around 11:00.
>
> So there ya go—my life.

Conner chimes in. "Truthfully, Pat, there's not much else to do, outside of some classes offered by some of the Montgomery churches or Auburn offering classes now and then . . . or you know, book clubs, like this one . . . oh, and we have a lot of church services, if you're into that kinda thing."

Talk turns, once again, to the state legislature trying to reform the prison system. Bits and pieces of information get passed on to my women. This causes hopes to soar one moment and be dashed the next. The on-going rumor, at present, is that long-term prisoners, like themselves, may have a chance to be reclassified and be eligible for work release or even parole. With the Alabama system at 192 percent of capacity—the most overcrowded in the country—my girls are convinced the system will want to purge them, just to cut down on the overload.

Yeah, right, I think to myself, but give a nodding smile.

Another rumor is that the warden is going to retire next year, and this is met with some vague apprehension because everybody seems to like the one we have now and no one knows what they might get as a replacement.

Refreshment time. I brought fruits: grapes, bananas, apples. They had told me they didn't get enough fruit in their daily diet, so I obliged. Betty, one of the long-long-timers, hailing from the Black Belt, had said that sometime she would love a banana sandwich for refreshment—just like when she was a girl and had them at her grandmama's house. She saved her banana to take back to her box and make one. (Mayo packs out of the vending machines and bread from . . . I didn't ask.) Betty reminds me of a woman Gomer Pyle. (Remember him from the old *Andy Griffith* TV show? A happy-go-lucky guy.) Betty is a happy-go-lucky girl, just going along to get along. A product of her small-town south Alabama heritage and proud of it. "I was in jail at home for three years, 'fore I took a plea bargain and ended up in here. Back home, I knew all the guards and my mama—she would bring me my meals most of the times."

Betty's big regret is that she left her two boys behind when she got sent here—talks about her boys constantly. She's in for murder and keeps being sent back to Tutwiler because she can't stay off the heavy drugs. Being in prison here is like living in Candyland if you're drug dependent. And of course, if you are drug dependent in here, your fellow inmates teach you all sorts of ways to fake passing the drug screenings. Testing positive for marijuana won't get you sent back to Tutwiler, but testing positive for the harder stuff will.

As I was leaving, I wished Rosalee good luck—not quite getting the marriage in prison thing but happy for Rosalee, who seemed quietly delighted.

On our way out this time, and being escorted by a guard, I noticed a concrete slab, cracked and worn, in the exercise yard and asked the girls if they would like to have a net and rackets to play a little tennis—something to do. All of them seemed enthusiastic. Conner said she could teach tennis to the others if I could get a few balls, a net, and some rackets. I've played tennis socially for a long time and knew I could get funding for the equipment from the U.S. Tennis Association. On a whim, I asked if the guard—happened to be a nice one—would escort me and Sara out to the exercise ground to take a look at what used to pass for a basketball court. Seemed plenty big enough for a small tennis court.

I decided I would email the warden and ask permission to bring in the equipment, thinking it would be a sport in which almost everyone could participate.

As we headed out of the parking lot, I asked Sara what she thought about bringing in tennis equipment. "After all, Sara, in here, the residents aren't exactly overwhelmed with things to do, and tennis would be a nice pastime for everybody."

"Sure it would," she said, giving one last look back at the barbed wire fencing as we drove out of the parking lot. "But remember, kiddo, I was a volunteer in one of the prisons up in New Jersey when Chris and I lived up there. It's not always as it seems, ya know."

CHAPTER 4

Wedding Bells

This month, Sara and I breezed through the gate with Ms. Foley and our goodies. No problem—non-searching guard.

Great. I'm thinking that all the trouble I went to gathering in ten used paperback copies of this read would be well worth it. I knew everyone would have enjoyed the first half, and we would discuss the last half next meeting. Big book and looks imposing, although it is not. I thought reading the life story of Katharine Graham—publisher of *The Washington Post*, a wealthy, well-connected woman who hobnobbed with the rich and famous but still had problems with her own self-confidence—would be fascinating to my group, because in time, she had reinvented the woman she was and had become independent and self-realized. It would be something they could identify with, since my ten had had plenty of their own struggles, although more rudimentary. Still, I think being timid and lacking confidence is a trait not confined to any economic or scholarly class.

And after all, *Personal History* had been on the best-seller list for months when it first came out—won a Pulitzer, among other prizes, and I had loved the book.

When we began our discussion of the book of the month, I was told that nobody had finished reading the first half, but everybody had the same opinion. They hated it.

Conner, being our leader, started the discussion. "What a snob the woman was." She began furiously flipping through pages trying to find a place that proved it.

"Too boring," Ms. Foley said. "I don't have no truck with none of them sorry politicians she been studyin'."

"I made it to chapter 4." Linda, the librarian, looked to the ceiling and groaned, "God, the woman had everything. What was she worried about? And if she didn't have it, she could buy it."

Conversely, Betty couldn't fathom—"So what's the big deal with, *poor Katharine* [fingers brandishing quote marks in the air] and all her money? I had money one time, lots of it, and hell, here I am."

Betty had been married to a man who worked on the oil rigs out in the Gulf of Mexico. He was killed in a drilling accident and she came into the insurance money. "Now *I* was *rich*, lemme tell ya. Bought my mama a house. Think it musta set me back more'n forty grand." Betty grimaced, remembering her past riches and her missteps in managing it. She sighed and leaned back in her chair. "The rest of it, I pissed away."

My sister Sara—having read the book of the month and knowing that *poor Katharine* was a multi-multi-millionaire who probably spent more than forty grand on her shoes each year—suddenly became fascinated with the linoleum floor, staring down at it, trying to hide the grin.

Ms. Foley sat shaking her head slowly, commiserating with poor Betty and her lost fortune.

I could see that perhaps their understanding of this read was a tad narrow and might not be relatable in the money category. I would try a different tack. I started reading excerpts from the first half of *Personal History*, which culminates with Katharine Graham's husband, Phil, committing suicide. As I read and paused to ask questions—especially when I asked if they had ever been mistreated by a man the way Graham's husband verbally abused her—the chatter ramped up.

"Is a bean green, honey?" Librarian Linda, with her misshaped arm and missing teeth, as a reminder of her past dealings with men. "Men can screw you over. Tell me about it. All men can screw you over, and sometimes I don't even think they mean to—just that ignorant."

"Why do you think I'm in here, Miss Pat? A man." Betty shakes her head, remembering. She had been with a man (this was after her first husband died on the oil rigs) who shot and killed an old lady they had attempted to rob. Betty says she was high and doesn't remember it, but she's fairly certain she didn't do it.

At this point Baby Cakes—a relatively timid member of our group—decided to enter into the discussion (it must have been the face that triggered the nickname—round and innocent-looking, like a baby doll's). This was a first because Baby Cakes was usually voiceless—had not said more than a yes or no in contribution in the entire time she had been in book club. Interesting how awakenings come at the most unusual times. Who knows what life experience triggered her outburst and brought forth the new Baby Cakes?

"I ain't impressed with *poor old Katharine Graham*," she mimicked. Someday, she said, she was going to write her own autobiography, and it would be way better than this one—she would go on TV and have a movie made. "And I'm gonna make mine *in-ter-est-ing*"—she drew it out again, "*in-ter-es-ting*, for the Lord's sake."

Baby Cakes is the youngest in our group, now that the younger members have gone back to Tutwiler. In her early thirties, I would guess—in for murder, fourteen years so far. Spurred on by her newfound voice, she kicked back her chair, stood up, and began to preach to us, "My motto is Veni Vidi Vici." She sighed, knowing she would need to explain. "It means, to all y'all that don't know it—it means, 'I came, I saw, I conquered'—and that's what I'm about." Baby Cakes continued, telling us how we should live our lives and what it takes—on her part—to do that, here in prison and throughout life. Our other members were patient, sitting back in chairs waiting for Baby Cakes to finish her tirade.

I glanced over to my sister, who was now staring down at her hands folded neatly in her lap, but she couldn't resist giving me a whispered aside. "*Ole Katharine's* probably rolling over in her grave about now."

"Very funny," I whispered back but didn't look at her for fear I might smile.

I was fast coming to realize that with any of our reads, we would start at our own jumping-off point, and not concern ourselves with other people's level of erudition—Right, Pat.

Sara's amusement aside, I still insisted that we take up the second half next time. I told everyone that if they couldn't stand to read it, to at least skim to the end. I am not going to leave a monthly read, no matter how negligible the group's understanding, or empathy, without some attempt at a finish.

Have I said that before?

Harriettee, who was sitting on my other side, turned to me and, probably as a way to help assuage my misstep with this read, said, "I remember my parents talking about the hoopla with *The Post* and the Watergate thing. We were stationed in Germany at the time."

Okay, so maybe one person had related.

Just as I was about to bring up another interesting point in the book—at least I thought it was interesting—the talk turned abruptly to Rosalee's wedding, and that immediately captured everyone's attention. Conner turned to Sara, and said in a half whisper, "I've got pictures to show you—of the wedding."

My problem was that at this point, I too was more interested in what happened at Rosalee's wedding than in poor Katharine's plight, and so . . . we rambled off course, as usual. Was it planned intervention on their part or just a case of group distraction?

It is as it is.

The wedding had taken place a week or so earlier, in the very room we were sitting in now. Metal tables had been pushed to the side to make room for the ceremony, stacks of old Bibles—leftovers from church meetings—had been lined up nicely in a waiting cabinet. Food and decorations were sprinkled about on the tables, streamers hung on walls. All said that Rosalee was a lovely bride—beautiful white flowing wedding gown. Her grandfather was in attendance. Later, I went online and saw the pictures on her new husband's Facebook page.

All the while, I was sitting there thinking to myself—There was wedding music? The groom wore full highlander dress—kilt and all? The guests were, most of them, in for murder or manslaughter? All this in a prison, in south Alabama, with a groom fresh from the British Isles? Sometimes I feel like I'm right in the middle of *Alice's Adventures in Wonderland.*

While I sat trying to get my bearings, Conner was proudly showing Sara the pictures she had taken. At this point you are saying to yourself, Perhaps there is a hidden agenda here on the part of the groom. I try not to judge—just listen.

In any event, the girls were all happy to see Sara again and loved that her hair was growing back. They know that she has health issues and much admired her for her ongoing fight with cancer. In times past, Sara has said to me, with a laugh, that they like her because she's the one person they know who's worse off than they are. The contrast in their lives is so obvious, and ongoing. I had not thought of it before—only that Sara had shown a great interest in them and seemed to connect with them from the beginning.

She's great to have because she sees things I don't as I am trying to stick to the agenda I've planned for each session—a source of great mirth for the whole group. "Everybody pay attention, Pat wants to finish her . . . [all together and hooting] ageeenda."

Of course, I never do—it's like herding . . .

I think, in their eyes, I couldn't be more square if I were a block of wood. I am the oddball in here, having never been in prison, never been arrested, having had loving, caring parents—haven't even gotten a speeding ticket—never smoked marijuana. Wait—I am that very block of wood. I must seem strange indeed to them. But they grow on me—and I think maybe I on them, but more than likely it's the refreshments.

Sara, on the other hand, lived in New Jersey before she and her husband retired and moved to the North Georgia mountains. In our little book club world, being from New Jersey automatically gives you a pass into worldly avarice, or at least into the knowledge of it. Sara is cool. She has a quiet self-confidence that is not at all diminished by her ongoing fight with cancer.

I don't mention to them that before she retired, Sara had been a vice president of tourism in Atlantic City—way too mundane.

Okay—time to give out the fluff. I always try to bring extra books and magazines—African American books for Baby Cakes and Maya—the two of them being great pals. You very seldom see one without the other. Actually, Maya shouldn't be in the book club at all, as it puts us over our ten limit when everyone is back here and in place. But then again, very seldom is everyone back here and in place as they should be—I let it slide.

This time, I brought them a copy of *The Emperor of Ocean Park*, along with several African American romance books. Maya—in for murder and driving under the influence—is more meticulous than most about what she reads—and what she eats. She prefers to sit back and listen. Rather than enter the conversation, she will usually let her pal Baby Cakes do the talking for both of them. Once, she did offer, "I killed somebody drunk driving and I'm in for murder, and Pammie, sittin' over there—Pammie did the very same thing and she's in for manslaughter—go figure that."

I glanced over to Pammie—actually it's Pamela but nobody calls her that—and for the first time I took a really good look at her. She smiled timidly and raised a finger in acknowledgment and I realized she had been with us the whole time but had hardly made an impression on me. I was to find out later on that that was exactly what she wanted—to be the cliché face in the crowd—going along to get along.

This time, toward the end of our session, when Val was recording the paperbacks, she had gathered a good assortment of gardening books to hand to Ms. Foley.

Again, Conner admonished, "I tell her she's too old to operate that heavy machinery, but she just laughs me off."

Ms. Foley took up her gardening books, preparing to leave. "Been usin' a tractor since before you was born, honey."

I said, "Rumor has it you may be up for parole, Ms. Foley." She frowned at me—and so did the others, glancing my way with terse looks. I had spoken out of turn. It's bad luck to presume a happy ending. But I couldn't help it. I could already see her sitting in a front porch rocker, smiling down on the flowers that line her front walk, in a little house on a backcountry road.

"I ain't countin' my chickens," she said, but I noticed a slight smile.

"What will they do without you around here to keep the place looking good, Ms. Foley?"

"I done told the warden, I'll train up somebody for him."

Refreshments: We had banana sandwiches—harkening back to Betty's childhood. I had brought loads of bananas, white bread, mayo, peanut butter, homemade banana bread (compliments of sister Joanne), and drinks. They dug in, especially Baby Cakes's pal, Maya, as the bananas are soft enough for her to be able to enjoy, given her facial scars—the result of the smashup that got her in here.

Another advantage of refreshment time at book club is this: Ordinary dinner time in this facility starts around 4:30 in the afternoon. It's served in rounds of about fifty people per session, fifteen minutes per session, as there is not enough room to serve more than that number in one sitting. So, inmates line up, go in and eat, and then they are rushed out to make room for the next group that's lined up in the hall, waiting. On book club day, they can skip their regular dinner, take their time and eat and talk and eat and eat and talk and talk and talk. Sometimes I think we are more group therapy club than book club. Maybe, to some extent, all book clubs are that way.

Prison grounds

CHAPTER 5
Christmas Cheer

Big news of the day: The head of the Alabama Department of Corrections has been fired and a new one appointed. Sometimes I am out of state between book club visits and have to skip a month and I don't get the latest prison news in a timely fashion, but this news was enough to foster hope. Change for the better might be in the works: that the population might be reduced from the three hundred who are packed in here now to something more manageable—that Ms. Foley might not have to move her bed away from the wall to keep from getting wet every time it rains—that there will be a full complement of guards to run the place—that . . . Well, we can always hope.

I didn't know it then, but I was to discover as time went on that in here, prison reform is a mirage dancing off in the distance, dangled down to them, and the general population, like a toy on a string—a hope to feed the illusion of progress.

Ms. Foley had greeted Sara and me at the gate with her white padded jacket pulled on over regular prison wear. Winter was upon us in the prison yard, and it showed in the brown dry windswept grass and bare flowerbeds. I supposed Ms. Foley and her assistants had spent hours pulling dried flowers and readying the ground for the coming year.

She was coughing as she talked. Told me it's a winter cold she gets this time of year. As an aside and in a whisper, she told me she had a parole hearing coming up next month. "But don't tell nobody, 'cause if it don't go through . . ."

I whispered back. "What a great way to start the new year, Ms. Foley." I had heard that being up for parole is usually something you keep to yourself, because if others have a grudge against you, they might be tempted to tell stories on you that could delay your hearing and maybe your release, although I could not imagine the Ms. Foley I know falling into that category.

The guards scurried in and out of the check-in office, which is not half warm to begin with, but better than the wind. South Alabama winters are short and not severe, if you gauge by the thermometer, but they come with a bone-chilling damp that penetrates everything. I had recently traveled to Montana where the temperature was twice as low but the feel was half as cold.

We unloaded with a fine mist settling in on us and then walked toward the visitation center. Nice to get into our book club room, close the door, and turn up the heat. There might even have been a little Christmas in the air, although no sign of it in the way of decorations. This meeting would be our little celebration of the coming Christmas season.

Despite the approaching holiday, everyone seemed grumpy, momentarily anyway. I was told that the hot water had been off for days and if you wanted to take an ice-cold shower, it'd be at your own risk. "Froze my tush off, yesterday when I tried it," Linda said as she pushed tables together for our session.

Ms. Foley: "And visitation's this weekend. You don't wanna be smelly."

Harriettee: "Talk about smelly. Dorm smells like a sewer, what with the toilets stopped up too."

Val, the accountant, is ever precise. "But only three of them—those three down on the very end of that row of ten, next to the wall. You can use the others—if you hold your nose."

Ms. Foley: "Holdin' your nose don't help. Smells just as bad over in the bunks as it does in them toilets. Don't make no mind if it's in the last three. Worse'n any outhouse I ever been in."

Val referenced an expert. "The girl in the bunk across from me, she used to be a restaurant manager, says it's because they hadn't cleaned out the grease trap in years. That's what does it—stops up everything. Says you could never get away with that if you was to run a restaurant."

"What does she know?" Ms. Foley scoffed. "She ain't been out in nigh-on to twenty year."

The whole conversation was losing any thought of the holiday spirit, so I tried to change the subject. "Sara came with me specially to see Conner and bring her some photography magazines she thought Conner would like."

Sara, smiling, held up her magazines, but the smile immediately faded as she looked to Ms. Foley. "Where is she?"

"You're outta luck on that account, Ms. Sara. She ain't gonna make it today."

Seemed both Conner and Rosalee were absent this time. Conner had to work in the laundry, as extra help was needed. She hoped she would be up for parole in the coming year and so wanted to do everything to move that process along—like no black marks for talk back and doing a good job of assigned tasks. She and the warden seemed to have a genial relationship—at least he knows who she is—so I was confident she had a chance—but what do I know? After all, as far as parole is concerned, the warden has very little to do with it.

Rosalee had a court date, or some such, to review her case. For the hearing, she had to travel back down to Dothan, Alabama, where she was arrested. I think it must be the work of her new English husband.

Oh well, maybe a few Christmas pictures would lighten the mood. I had asked permission—and it was given—to bring in a camera, so the expert, Sara, could take Christmas pictures. I said to the assembled that if they didn't want to be in the picture that was fine. I thought for sure there would be a few who would opt out. Surprisingly, all of them wanted to be in the group. They were happy to sign the release form. We got several cute shots of all the gang with paper Christmas hats Sara and I had brought in.

By now, most had evolved into a festive mood. Even Maya seemed a little happier than usual, although you can never tell with Maya. Because of her facial injury—a big scar down the side of her face—she never changes expression. And she always sits at the opposite end of the discussion table with her pal, Baby Cakes. Usually, Baby Cakes answers all the questions put to that end of the table during discussion time with Maya looking on and nodding. Maya is, would be, a beautiful woman, if not for the accident. She appears to me to be a mix of white and Black with perhaps some Hispanic influence.

Our book discussion this time was secondary to this meeting because, of course, they still did not approve of poor Katharine Graham's personal history—"still boring." Harriettee and Ms. Foley had finished it, but they were the only ones. Although Pammie seemed to be the fastest reader in our group, she hadn't finished either. If, on occasion, I am not able to get enough books to go around, Linda will say, "Give one to Pammie first and she'll finish it overnight and pass it on."

Upon first meeting Pammie, your eye passes right by as there is nothing much to distinguish her. She is rather chunky—okay, fat—with this pasted half smile that says, "Don't pick me for anything"—and you don't, until you get to know her and realize she is the one who has learned to game the system and live her own life inside these walls, amid all the ongoing disorder.

After the rather hostile reception I had gotten last month with Katharine Graham's read, I told them we would change the format this time and that two people would be chosen, or volunteer, to be the presenters for this last half of Katharine Graham's book.

I had thought that maybe this would encourage more participation and put the responsibility of presentation on them. Maybe it would encourage the presenters to read the books more thoroughly and think about what they had read. Conner and Rosalee had volunteered for this first presentation. Now both were absent. It is the way of book club in here. You can never tell who might be absent on a given day, but we go with the flow. If it had to happen, I supposed that this was as good a time as any, as the girls never could get into Katharine Graham, or have much empathy for her life story.

I had recently read a couple of books about writing your autobiography and got the idea that the book club members might like to write theirs. I asked if they would like to try writing an autobiography—kind of an ongoing book club assignment we might start.

They were horrified.

Linda: "My God, Pat. What are you thinking? I can't write. Besides,

I don't have a typewriter; sure as hell I don't have access to a laptop. I wouldn't even know where to begin. The last computer course I had was in old-timey DOS."

Uma: "Yeah, whatcha think—we John Grisham or somebody?"

"What about if I bring you a pencil and notebook and give you a series of questions about your life and you answer them and then when you finish all the questions—ta-da! You have your autobiography."

There was an immediate collective sigh.

Pammie: "Well, why didn't you say so? We can all answer questions. Why, fuck, anybody can do that . . . I mean, *heck*, anybody can do that. Sorry, Miss Pat."

Even Betty seemed interested now, momentarily shaking off her drug-induced glazed look. "I have had some interesting times in my life . . . and my boys might enjoy readin' . . . Yeah, why not?"

And now for Christmas cheer—Chick-fil-A sandwiches and fries, tea and Christmas cupcakes, on Christmas themed paper plates. The girls always bring their own drink filled with ice from the ice machine, and this time of year, they pull a sock around the container to keep their fingers from freezing.

And gifts. Sara had brought little offerings of hand lotion, lip balm, and small packets of instant flavoring for their water. And in anticipation of the coming autobiographies, I had brought journals for each one to write in, answering questions about their lives.

The atmosphere had finally turned cheery. I even thought of suggesting we might all sing a Christmas carol or two, but come to think of it, perhaps a bridge too far. Besides, we had one other surprise in store.

CHAPTER 6

Tennis, Almost, Anyone?

After we had finished with our refreshments and Christmas favors, I announced that we were to adjourn to our new tennis court. The warden had given me permission, so this time I had brought the tennis equipment the girls said they wanted—courtesy of the U.S. Tennis Association, as I have been a longtime volunteer with the organization. Everyone was excited at the prospect of something new and rushed back to their bunks to store their Christmas goodies. I got a guard to escort us—Sara and me—out to our new court to take a look. The girls rushed out to join us. Although it was chilly, and rather windy, we got out the new net to test it on the concrete pad the girls had cleared of weeds. It worked fine, with the exception of a few odd bounces from the many holes and cracks in the surface. We used old balls as the new livelier ones might bounce over the razor wrapped barbed wire fencing and be gone.

Harriettee said that she would like a friend of hers—not in book club—to be our guest next book club meeting. She's a long-timer and had helped them as they were cleaning up the court surface—down on her hands and knees, picking out all the weeds that had seeped through the cracks over the years. "She hasn't got any money in her account, so she can't get any canteen stuff. I know we can't offer money, but we could offer free refreshments."

Linda: "She's a little on the burned brain side, but she did work hard with us."

"Great. Next meeting, I'll bring extra refreshments for her."

I realized I would have to find some way to line the court later on, but I was so pleased thinking that this would be an activity in which everyone in the prison could participate—spring, fall, and winter. Maybe not so much during the hottest summer months.

Linda, Harriettee, Sara, and I sat and talked for a while as we watched the others rallying on our makeshift court with some success and much enthusiasm.

I had recently read an article about the effects of early childhood trauma on subsequent adult life, so of course I couldn't resist asking, as I was sitting there with primary source material. Most of my group had said that they had had, in one way or another, a traumatic childhood. "What do y'all think is most traumatizing for a child?"

Harriettee, our reformed user, looked to the heavens and shook her head. She took out a small metal box that held her newly rolled cigarettes, got one out, and prepared to light up. "Pat, darlin', you don't mess with that subject in here." She took a long drag and let out the smoke slowly. "When I first came in, they heard I used to be a teacher and they thought I might be in for molesting a child." She took another drag. "Had to show them my time sheet to prove I was in for drug trafficking."

She turned to Linda. "Remember that?"

Linda nodded. "We were just making sure you were who you said you were."

Sara: "Can't blame ya."

We watched as one of the girls tripped going for a fast ball and the others walked over to help her up. Smoke from cigarettes on the small bleachers adjacent to the court drifted up into the afternoon air as the sun headed down into pines. At this one moment we could have been sitting in a public park anywhere—perhaps without all the drifting cigarette smoke.

I decided to venture another question. "What would y'all think about having a book club for the illiterate short-termers in here? We could use books on tape, or CDs, or some equivalent. Books on tape and CDs are a dime a dozen now that there are so many other ways to read." I had thought it would be a productive way to pass the time. Something they could do and I would help organize, but immediately they were dismissive.

Linda: "The short-termers aren't interested in anything uplifting—really, Pat."

Harriettee: "They read mostly—if they read at all—sex and porn stuff."

Linda: "Pat, you have to realize, most of these short-timers in here are lowlife criminals with no values—no morals whatsoever."

Sara took a sudden interest in the lovely sunset, not daring to comment.

I nodded slowly—and no, I did not point out the obvious.

Just then, one of the short-termers—a young girl who looked to me to be about seventeen at the most—ventured over. I'm sure she must have been older. She was one of the forty or fifty other inmates who were sitting on a grassy area next to the dorm, smoking and watching our tennis progress.

"I was just wondering—I'm new here, from Louisiana . . . and uh . . . and I love to read . . . especially books set in Louisiana." She smiled. If she had had a hat, it would have been in hand.

"Really." Harriettee gazed out over the exercise yard, never condescending to make eye contact.

Encouraged, Louisiana continued. "I was just wondering . . . if you ever have an opening . . . in the book club . . . I was just wondering." She hesitated again and then added, "And I play a pretty good game of tennis too."

Harriettee glanced at Linda. They both sighed—in unison—as if having just heard the most idiotic suggestion imaginable, and then turned to look at Louisiana.

Harriettee: "Did you *kill* anybody?"

Taken aback but hoping that it would be a point in her favor, Louisiana smiled timidly, "No, I never . . . I'm not in for something like that."

It sealed her fate. For the first time, Harriettee looked Louisiana full in the face, eyes narrowing into menacing slits. "What in the world makes you think you can join? Beat it."

Poor Louisiana began taking slow steps backward, her audience ended.

Me: "What did you say that for? You're not in for murder. You're in for drugs and you scared the kid half to death."

She and Linda began to snicker. I began to feel like Louisiana. "Really, Pat. That's the point, girl. No way they can use our stuff."

Sara, grinning at all the crossfire, immediately fell into the chiding. "Yeah, Pat, the hoi pollois can't associate with us—really, girl."

So much for my idea of a sport of universal participation.

※

After a while, Sara and I, along with Ms. Foley, were escorted back to the meeting room and began packing up to leave. I looked over to Ms. Foley and gave her a thumbs-up. Then I walked over and hugged her, thinking I might never see her again.

On our way out, as we—me, Sara, Ms. Foley, and the guard—walked past the big Butler-like building that houses all the bunkbeds, toilets, and showers, the heavy stench of raw sewage drifted along with us on our pathway to the gate. Betty appeared out of a side door and began accompanying us and whispered, "Smelled so bad, I called my mama and my mama she got so mad she up and called the fire department and told 'em it was a emergency. Peoples could die in here."

"Good for her," Sara said, fanning the stench away from her face. We stood at the gate now waiting for the buzzer to go off and let us out. "Did they come—the fire trucks?"

"Come—but the warden wouldn't let 'em in."

"Bummer, but a good try," Sara said and high-fived Betty just as the gate buzzer went off.

Sara opened up the back door of my van and I threw in our empty boxes and books returned from last month's read. "That was creative of the mama. Didn't do any good, but it was creative."

"Yeah." I couldn't help but laugh. "Wonder what the guards thought when the fire engines came roaring up, sirens blasting away?"

It had been dark for a good half hour when Sara and I drove out of the parking lot in our cozy warm minivan—heater blasting away. Christmas music from a Montgomery radio station swirled around us. A crescent moon was swinging through gathering clouds as we pulled onto I-85 going north. Headlights of the big eighteen-wheelers destined for Atlanta reflected back the first drops of rain that had begun to fall. I knew some of my gang would have relatives that would come to visit—some would not. Some, like Ms. Foley, would be sitting on their bunks, imagining that this time next year, they might be on parole and spending the holiday on the outside. Sara and I were headed to a big family gathering with husbands and wives, sisters and brothers, uncles and aunts, children and grandchildren.

Later in the month we received Christmas cards from some of the group. In addition to enjoying the lovely sentiments, it is the expense involved in sending a card (the stamps and the cards themselves, which some can ill afford) that made Sara and me truly appreciate their efforts.

Dearest Sara, You are the best! Please know that my prayers are with you for a very merry Christmas and a prosperous, happy and HEALTHY new year.

God Bless!

With Love, Harriettee

Thank you for taking the time to come to us with books, joy and games.

Love you, Baby Cakes and Maya

To Pat

Thank you for accepting me and I know I took ——s place but I see that you asked about her. I was amazed. You know what she did, yet you didn't judge her. That was the greatest thing ever! I'm sure you are a great upscale lady like Katharine Graham (ha ha ha) It was nice to see that you really see the good in people.

Thanks, Uma

Christmas and a New Year of happiness!

Pammie

Merry Christmas,

Della Foley

Sara, Merry Christmas! I hope this holiday season brings with it happiness for you and yours. You are such a special precious person in my life. I'm grateful and privileged to call you friend.

Merry Christmas,

Conner

CHAPTER 7
No Parole

Damp, cold, and cloudy with a slight mist falling—just enough to coat our hair, jackets, pants. To my eyes, the weather seems to be the only thing that changes the look of this place. In the winter, gray buildings and gray lawns. In the summer, gray buildings with green lawns and, of course, Ms. Foley's flowerbeds. Now they were mounded circles of earth out in the yard and along the sidewalks, waiting.

And there she was, waiting, pulling her cart down the sidewalk toward the fence. She greeted me with a nod and what might have been a tight smile. The guard in the reception office punched a buzzer that unlocked the gate for her. Sara was not with me this time, as our meeting date had conflicted with one of her chemo treatments.

We walked to the back of my car—the escort guard following. As I lifted the tailgate of my minivan, I said, "Ms. Foley, I was hoping . . ."

"Had an objector," she mumbled as she heaved one of the heavy boxes full of paperbacks out of the trunk.

I grabbed a plastic sack full of old magazines. "Oh, Ms. Foley, I'm . . . sorry."

"Lyin' about me, she was. Says I wrote to her terrible things . . . and I never."

Trying not to let my disappointment show, I took up another plastic bag of old magazines and pitched it onto the cart. The bag ripped and scattered magazines all over the ground, some under my van. We went down on our hands and knees picking up the remains. I whispered to her, "Is there anything you can do?" It was a lame question—more of a condolence.

This was the first time I had been around when a member of our book club was up for parole and didn't get it, and it caught me off guard. Through the years I would watch the process unfold countless times. Each time there is a no-go I have to catch myself. More specifically, I have to catch my thinking. In here, it's so easy to forget the flip side of the coin. What of the lost lives their foolish, and sometimes malicious, actions had precipitated? And how their one act will inevitably cascade down through coming generations touching hundreds of lives—children, grandchildren, great . . . Our atomic chain reaction, of the human kind. "*My mama never knew her mama—never had no idea how to raise me . . . or care for me. She was mad at the world from the get-go.*" I have heard that or variations on that statement times too numerous to count.

Simultaneous to my coming, and while we were waiting for the gate to open and let us in, we watched as a work-release van pulled up, letting off workers at another gate. They got a quick check from the guards to make sure there was no contraband. There is loads of it, I am told.

I was still thinking about Ms. Foley's bad news when the guard office buzzed the gate to let us in. Our escorting guard this time, a white guy, was a serious one—never a smile—the telltale mark of a newbie. He went through every book and every magazine, almost page by page, and did a thorough check of the refreshments. I figured he must be new or maybe this treatment was the result of what, I was later told, went on a few days before my coming. Seems that one of the inmate van drivers who took inmates to work and back every day had been bringing in drugs as a way to supplement her income. According to my gang, the guards came and got the driver's mattress in the middle of the night and put her in a room by herself until she gave up her stash, obviously in body cavities—or they would have waited until they got a warrant for a body search.

While we were crossing the yard, heading to our meeting room, we ran into a new girl—new to me anyway. She seemed eager to help us move in books and food. She said she would love to join the book club, that she loved to read. It was her life's passion. Ms. Foley rolled her eyes but still was kind to the woman, thanking her for her help with some books that had fallen off the cart. When we got inside and I told the others about her, they gagged—said she was a looney and they would not have her join for anything. "Pat, really, we're exclusive," Conner said, raised her eyebrows, and grinned, "exclusive as you can get in here."

As we were setting up, I realized that several people were missing—specifically Harriettee and Uma, and they were the very two who had volunteered to give the book report this time. My new idea to share responsibility for reporting on the book was out the window.

I looked to Conner for enlightenment. "Sorry, Pat, but Harriettee got called back to Dothan, where she was first arrested. Has a court hearing there. She's trying to get eligible for outside work."

"Okay, can't help that. Where's Uma?"

"Well, now, Uma, she was sent to Tutwiler last week for getting in a dust-up with one of the guards."

"What is it with Uma?" I couldn't do anything but shake my head and pass out paper plates.

You can just look at Uma and know she will not take anything from a guard who's trying to throw their weight around, especially because she's been in here since most of the guards were children—no way. I can't help but like her spunk. The system will never, ever get her down. She reminds me of a John Wayne character in the old-time Western movies. Just throw it at me, baby, I can take it—and in addition, she usually figures a way for her depravity to work to her advantage—but always with a smile.

I started placing napkins on our makeshift grouping of tables and turned to Val, who was checking in her pockets for her pen to mark MWF on book spines, identifying all the books I had brought in. "I hate to lose Uma. Hope this won't mean she's gone from here for good."

Val, finding her pen and beginning to mark, said, "Oh, no. I think she'll be back. Everybody knows that guard she was messing with is a real ass. Maybe by the time you come next month, she'll be back—maybe."

Ms. Foley: "We all know him. He ain't worth foolin' with."

While Harriettee was in Dothan trying to get a different classification, Rosalee was just back from the Dothan jail, where she also had a hearing, and she began to speak up about it—which was unusual for Rosalee. "The worse place I have ever been in," she said in a quiet voice, shivering and hugging herself. "I couldn't brush my teeth for two days and I had to stay in the same clothes for that length of time too. Nobody could say a thing or they would be sent to seg. It's that strict."

Val chimed in. "Tell about the toilets. You think our toilets are bad."

Rosalee: "Oh, yes. The toilets are only allowed to be flushed every three hours and if you need to buy something and don't have the money, like if you needed a pad for your period—you had to show that you were . . . staining, to get one." Rosalee shook her head. "I hate to say I love being back in here, but at least in here, you can get those . . . uh . . . necessities, when you need them." Rosalee—ever the delicate one.

Conner: "Okay, okay—enough. I'm losing my appetite. Let's get on with it."

Me: "And speaking of Tutwiler, where's Betty?" While Rosalee was telling of her Dothan adventures, I had been looking around for Betty.

Conner: "I was gonna tell you about that. She got sent back again. Got caught with drugs because somebody snitched on her."

Me: "Well, where'd she get them—again?"

Conner: "Hello—she bought them. Whatcha think?"

It occurred to me—maybe the prison van driver? I'm only speculating. At various times I have been told that there is a rather large drug ring in here and a variety of preparations are available—for a price.

Me: "So even though half the group is missing, we can still get on with our book of the month. What did you think was the . . . ?"

Conner: "There's one other thing I need to tell you about."

I leaned back in my chair, ready to give up, and we hadn't even gotten started. "Now what?"

Conner: "It's about Maya."

"What about Maya? Is she having trouble with that facial scar? It does look swollen and angry from time to time." I looked around. "She's not here either, I see. I just thought she might be late." I looked to Baby Cakes, Maya's constant companion, and expected an explanation from her, but she waved me off, on the verge of tears.

Linda took up the story. "Yeah, well, this is the sad part."

And I was thinking, Our other news wasn't sad enough? Ms. Foley denied parole—Betty back in Tutwiler—Uma in a dust-up with a guard, and now Maya?

Linda: "Maya's sixteen-year-old daughter was killed in a car wreck a few days back. Her family came up from Mobile to tell her about it and the warden—with a judge's approval of course—had a deputy take her down to the funeral.

Conner: "She got a twenty-four-hour pass, which I thought was nice."

"I'm so sorry. What a shock to Maya. That's so sad."

And I was thinking to myself—as I'm sure some of the others were—how ironic in a way, in that she was in here herself for traffic violations that turned deadly. I leaned back in my chair, suddenly realizing that all the other mishaps of the month seemed trivial in comparison to losing a child. "And yes," I said as I came back to the moment, "it was nice of the warden to let her go."

Conner: "She was in the back seat, so they said. She and another kid."

Linda: "I was in charge of taking up money for travel expenses and to help out with the funeral expenses."

I had not imagined there would be enough cash circulating in here to help with funeral expenses. Evidently, I was wrong—as usual. "I'm so sorry to hear that. I know she must be . . . devastated." The others commiserated with heads down.

I waited a moment more for another shoe to drop and when it didn't, I got on with introducing our book of the month. And it was the bright note—the one bright note so far, for this session.

The ones who were left all loved reading *Sarah's Key*. Said it kept them turning pages. Another best seller that's off the best-seller list now so I got a bargain. It's set in Paris during World War II. You probably read it—sold millions. Sarah, a ten-year-old girl, is arrested, with her family, by the French police, but not before she locks her younger brother in a cupboard in the family's apartment, thinking she'll be back within a few hours to retrieve him.

Another historical novel. It's the old history teacher in me. I can't resist.

Linda said she read it all in one night.

All who were there said they read it and loved it but didn't like the ending. Harming a child seems always to be so overwhelming to them that everything else pales.

Most have said, in discussions past, that they were abused as children. And yet in later discussions, some of those same women have said that they were spoiled as children. Upon reflection, I suppose the two are not necessarily antithetical.

And Val, out of left field, says, "And another thing. When are we gonna get our autobiography questions that you were talking about? I've had several ideas about mine that I might want to include."

By now I have learned to go with the flow, and so I reached into my satchel and pulled out the first eleven questions for them to answer to begin their autobiographies. I noticed that Ms. Foley didn't take a sheet of questions as they were passed around. The others took theirs and seemed pleased with the prospect, immediately scanning the list, lost in their own thoughts, I suppose, considering answers.

My sister Joanne has volunteered to type up and print out the answers to their questions—make it look more official. My hope is that we will eventually have enough to compile an autobiography for each member—with a cover and everything. Nothing fancy, but something to show for their life, something they can have in hand—their life thus far.

We continued with our discussion of the book of the month with Val, Linda, and Conner doing most of the talking. The others passively listened while sneaking a glance now and then at their list of autobiography questions.

All through our meeting, I felt I should have said something more to Ms. Foley about her refused parole. Toward the end of our get-together, when everyone was busy selecting used paperbacks, I asked Conner, "What about Ms. Foley? Will she ever . . ?"

"Probably not."

I pulled Conner aside on the pretense of helping me pack up. My curiosity was getting the best of me. "There's something I've been wondering about, but I hesitate to ask Ms. Foley for fear it might upset her more than she is already."

Conner smiled her benevolent smile at me. "Shoot. If I don't know the answer, I'll make one up."

"Very funny. But honestly, tell me. With all she has told me about her, uh . . . offense that put her in here, and I know she pleaded guilty like everybody else, but why is she in for capital murder? Didn't she have a chance to plead manslaughter—after all, he had a gun and was gonna shoot her—or maybe plead some other lesser degree because, she's told me, she was taking so many drugs for depression at the time she shot him? She coulda pleaded temporary insanity—maybe."

Conner pitched some remaining pencils in my take-out box and shook her head. "Beats me. Must be some kind of lawyer thing. We've talked about that. Some time back, one of the women in here—one that has some training in law—helped Ms. Foley make up a case for an appeal, but I don't think it went anywhere. You know lawyers. After they talk, and talk, and talk, you don't know whether you're coming or going."

Before Conner turned to leave, she said, "You know, you people on the outside, you can go to the place she was sentenced and get a copy of the court records. It's public knowledge. Course it'll cost you a pretty penny. Probably not worth the effort."

We finished the indoor portion of our book club and went out to the exercise yard.

I had borrowed—from a high school coach I know—a gizmo that lines football fields and baseball diamonds. We'd use it to put down lines for our makeshift court. The surface is so coarse, I was only hoping it would hold the imprint of the lines.

Linda and Pammie began popping a few lines with chalk and string I had brought—not particularly straight and not regulation but good for our purposes. Now if they would just stay in place for a while, our dandy little tennis court would be ready to go.

Another innovation. I brought more balls, an extra net, and some more rackets—for the "lowlife" short-termers. Now they will have their own equipment and be able to play—during those times when my ten aren't ruling the roost—which is almost never.

Across the yard we could see a van full of inmate day workers pull up and let off its load. Theoretically, most inmates here are supposed to be working on the outside during the day, but most of them aren't. I would judge, from what I see, only a relatively small number get to go outside the walls and work. Out of the three hundred or so in here right now, maybe twenty-five or thirty go outside to jobs. The number fluctuates. What originally started as a work-release facility has become—it appears to me—a dumping ground for all sorts and types of lawbreakers, from short-termers to revolving-door unhoused people to major felons to myriad burned brains.

I looked it up one time. There are ninety-plus towns in Alabama that have a population of three hundred or less. Suppose all the people in each of those towns came together each night to sleep in a space the size of a basketball court—I'm not saying these inmates don't deserve to be here. I'm just saying.

CHAPTER 8

Uma's April Fool

This time, while at the check-in booth, handing over my keys and driver's license before being escorted in, I got what must be a newbie guard who was answering the phone, trying to sweep out the place, then answering the phone again, then recording my entry—doing the job of three people, in vain. I waited.

Finally, she put down the phone and said, "Okay, let's check you out." Evidently, she had been given a new procedure to follow while checking volunteers in. She took me into the adjacent bathroom and began her inspection—having me pull out my pocket linings, then lift up my shirt, and asking me to shake out my bra, and then the phone rang again and she stepped out to answer it and was about to come back to me, but it rang again and she turned to answer and make a quick announcement over the PA and by that time there was another person on another line. After a couple more calls, I finally came out of the bathroom and pointed to my satchel and the books, thinking she would search them when she had a minute. She looked up from the phone and said, with a wave of the hand, "Oh, go ahead on in."

As I was picking up my stuff, and there was not a phone ringing for that moment, I asked, "So, Officer . . . Wiggins [a quick look at her nametag], it looks like y'all might be shorthanded today."

"Well, if people would just show up for work," says Officer Wiggins.

"Now that this new man has taken over the state's Department of Corrections, it'll be interesting. Maybe things will improve, with staffing I mean."

"Yeah," she turned to catch another ringing phone—"if they'll stop hirin' their kin that come in and get themselves promoted and don't do nothin'. I hope that'll change."

✳

As soon as Ms. Foley and I were inside the gate—sans officer escort this time (shorthanded again?)—here came Harriettee doing a dance across the grounds, rushing up to me and grinning, "Next time you come, you'll see me in street clothes."

High-five. "Get out of here. You got permission to work outside?"

"Yes, yes, yes," she said, giving me a hug. We all walked inside, chatting about her possible job opportunities.

This was going to be a good meeting. As we began to put out plates and books, I noticed Rosalee sitting quietly in her chair, not helping, not talking, staring straight ahead, a pasted look of acceptance. I remembered that a few months back she had been to Dothan to try and get a change in her classification.

I turned to all-knowing Conner—"The judge wouldn't even entertain a change in her status. She's back to square one. Bet that new husband of hers is miffed."

Conner tossed some paper plates to Linda to arrange around the table, then caught my eye and whispered: "While I, on the other hand, believe I have a parole hearing coming up some time soon—don't know when yet, but soon."

Another high-five.

The yin and the yang.

On to the book of the month. Last meeting, as a prerequisite to this month's novel, I had read them the United Nations definition of a hermaphrodite, then had given out the book—*Middlesex*. Although today the preferred designation is "intersex," "hermaphrodite" was used in this story so I went with that. It's about, among other things, a man who is born with an intersex condition and the life he and generations of his family lead as they migrate to America. Another best seller, and Pulitzer Prize winner, not that Pulitzer implies universal appeal—far from it.

With so much going on—parole, no parole, trips to classification hearings—only two people had finished *Middlesex*. You can guess who—but I do believe it was an instrument of learning. Well, that was my hope anyway. As it turned out, they knew more about the subject from the ground level than I did.

As we sat finishing up dessert, we talked about what intersex conditions are and how they come about—rather upsetting to the more traditional among us.

"I don't like to read about incest." Ms. Foley's understanding. She had slogged through the whole novel, and although it was alien to her philosophy of life, she was very understanding of the character and his plight. "Well, it wasn't his fault," she said.

Harriettee was the other one who had completed the read, and she seemed to have enjoyed it. "I liked his writing style. Can you imagine trying to write all of that family history and have the characters migrate to America at the same time? Must have taken him years."

Everyone else had an opinion, not necessarily based on the book, but an opinion nonetheless. They wanted to talk about Oak—that's her name, Oak. Not Oak Tree, just Oak. It seems that Oak was an inmate here in this prison for quite a while before she got transferred up to the women's facility in Birmingham, where they have private showers—no shower curtains here—and my group knew all about her—especially Uma, of course.

And yes, Uma is back from Tutwiler and she had some definite opinions about the novel and about inmate Oak, but first, we needed to hear a short rundown of Uma's Tutwiler sojourn. Actually, the rundown was meant for me because I wanted to know, and the others already knew, about what had gone on at Tutwiler the terrible.

Seems that in this instance the guard who had sent Uma back to Tutwiler had been caught telling lies about Uma and other inmates who had come in contact with him. This time there was a hearing and there were witnesses—Uma was one, she said—and he was finally caught red-handed. There were smiles of satisfaction on all the faces around our table. Uma was delighted that justice had triumphed and that she had been one of its vessels—not that she herself is an innocent when it comes to offenses.

We heard about how a hearing was held and that the offending guard was shown the door. As I sat there remembering how shorthanded the corrections department is to begin with, I realized the offending guard must really have been *offending*.

If there is a role model to the other members in here, it's Uma. No matter that Uma has been known to be involved in the drug trade in here, maybe big time. She seems to always go her own way, even if under the circumstances that might get her further jail time—and sometimes does. If it's wrong in Uma's eyes, it's wrong.

I sat listening to the tale of Uma's latest encounter with a system of law being imposed on this inside culture—from the outside. To my nerdy mind's eye, there seems to be a whole different moral universe in here, and sometimes I am hard-pressed to condemn it. I am reminded of Margaret Meade's study of, what to us would be, aberrant cultures. Their rules are built on the necessity of their circumstances, and in here, this culture works for these people, in these circumstances.

"Y'all finally nailed him," Conner was saying, of the guard. Everyone smiled.

After hearing about Uma's Tutwiler time, the talk drifted back to the book of the month and former fellow inmate Oak. It seemed that now Uma and the others had determined that Oak might have had an intersex condition.

Uma: "I wanted—I tried—to get into the showers at a time when Oak was in there so I could see for myself just what peoples was talkin' 'bout, but her friends—Oak's friends—wouldn't let me. Guarded that shower every time she took one."

Everyone seemed to know Oak, so maybe from now on their newfound knowledge would temper understanding. Who knows? I have long ago stopped trying to relate the two. You can only put knowledge out there, but so many times, it's overwhelmed by environment—like Baby Cakes. This read seemed to bring forth another of Baby Cakes's Veni Vidi Vici moments—not that she had read the book, of course, but she did have some conclusions about the whole thing. Pushing back her chair to give plenty of room for pontification, she said, "Now here's what I'm thinkin' 'bout ole Oak. If it had been me I woulda said, 'What y'all talkin' 'bout? I am like I am and don't nobody think 'bout changin' me.'" She nodded her head in agreement with herself. "She was queer, and she was showin' queer, and that's what I know 'bout it."

*

While we had been discussing the book of the month, Ms. Foley was sitting and listening and trying to keep from scratching. She had developed shingles. She thought it was shingles, but the prison nurse said it wasn't shingles because, she told Ms. Foley, one cannot have shingles on one's face. I didn't want to openly question that diagnosis, so I just said, "I believe you have shingles too, Ms. Foley." Ms. Foley was convinced that it surely was shingles, and so were the rest of us—we thought probably due to the stress of the parole hearing not going well. She was very tired and looked washed-out, with the red rash covering large parts of her body. She already had heart surgery in here—a few years back, I am told. We were all hoping she wouldn't overdo it. Still, she tended her flowers.

Linda: "Remember when Big Lacy had shingles and she kept everybody for three bunks around awake at night tossing and turning and scratching?"

The conversation was becoming more and more scattered at this point, which it usually does, so Conner called on Uma once again. "Tell us that story you were telling me this morning, Uma. After all, it's April." (Okay, it was not actually April, but close to it, and I wanted to hear the story, so I didn't object.) Any story Uma tells is worth listening to.

Uma grinned and took the floor.

"Well, all and all it wasn't funny," she said, clearing her throat in order to give the story more gravity. "Happened a few years back."

The others perked up, all ears. "Tell us, girl."

"Well, it was like this." Uma leaned back in her chair and took a sip of Coke. "See, I woke up on April Fool's Day, and I got up out of my bunk and I just plopped right down on the floor, like I was flat-out dying."

The others began to snicker.

"Now everybody else know what a kidder I am and they didn't pay me no mind—smilin' they just walk on past me like it was the middle of the day, like there was a big rock lying there in the middle of the floor, but the new guard on duty—she didn't know, so she commences gettin' real upset and runs over to me, bendin' down over me, and was just about to use her shoulder radio to call for help when I pops up and says, 'April Fools.'"

Gales of laughter.

"But now, hold on," Uma said. "That ain't the end of the story. The new guard don't like being shamed like that, so she calls her boss on her radio and she say her boss mad as a hornet. Told the guard to bring me on up to the office right then—actin' the fool like that. She say it irresponsible of me. So I went on up to the office and when I gets to the office the lieutenant in charge says that was inconsiderate and foolish of me to play a trick like that on the new guard, it being her first day on the job, and for that she was gonna be sendin' me back to Tutwiler."

"Tutwiler? For that? You're kidding!" Harriettee and the others were stunned at this turn in the story.

"And I'm sayin' to the lieutenant, 'What are you talkin' 'bout, Lieutenant—just a joke.'

"She say, 'Go on back to the dorm and change to your whites and pack your things and get ready for transport. No sense in you actin' out thata way, scarin' the new guard. Got enough trouble keepin' 'em as it is.'"

"My heavens," Rosalee said. "You were just kidding!"

"I know. I know. Crazy, right?" Uma shrugged. "So, I say to the lieutenant, 'You gotta be funnin' me.' She say, 'No back talk or you're gonna end up in seg.' She say, 'You heard me—go on.'"

At this point in the story, I was beginning to be concerned too, knowing Uma and her propensity not to back down.

Ms. Foley said, "You didn't do nothin' but play a joke."

"I know it. Couldn't believe she was sendin' me back to Tutwiler just for playin' a joke, but I went on back to the dorm and told the others and started to get my things together. The girls in the other bunks was standin' round feelin' terrible for me 'cause it was just a joke and wasn't fair for me to get sent back for a joke.

"I was mad too, but wasn't nothin' I could do about it so, I change to my whites—everybody standing around sorry for me—packed up my stuff and told everybody goodbye and went on back to report to the lieutenant, thinking, am I gonna be back there for another three months or what—maybe six months?

"So there I am standin' in the lieutenant's office, all packed up and ready to go—got my whites on.

"And the lieutenant stops what she's doin', looks up at me from her desk grinnin' and says to me . . . 'April Fools, Uma.'"

There was a collective groan. We all looked at each other—shaking heads and smiling. Duped by Uma—again.

"Oh, shit." Linda grinned, took some slivers of ice out of her cup, and threw them at Uma.

Uma, smiling, shrugged. "Not funnin' ya, that's what happened."

Conner, the one who had asked her to tell the story in the first place, slapped the table, laughing. "Got all y'all from the get-go."

Prison humor.

At this point, I supposed things were so upbeat that Conner proceeded to announce to the assembled that she would be coming up for a parole hearing in a month or two. Everyone began to congratulate her, saying it was about time. The general consensus seemed to be that she would make it this time. She had been in so long—sixteen years—and had a good record. Never mind that it's bad luck to announce it publicly like that. I assumed there must be exceptions to that rule, and this was one of them? Her sentence—I had looked it up on the Alabama Department of Corrections website—is for forty years, murder and attempted murder, but then again, what do I know. So much of life is wishful thinking—and in here, a prerequisite to survival.

Maybe it was the spring weather; everyone seemed happy and hopeful. Well, except for Rosalee, but we all knew her court hearing would be a long shot in the first place. I suppose her new husband wanted her to try it.

Even Linda came over to me and whispered that she would love it if I could write a letter of commendation for her library duties and tell about how much she has helped with correspondence in the book club. She hoped to use it in what might be an upcoming parole hearing of her own. I said I would, and would send it next week.

As we were finishing up, Baby Cakes said she had another person who had asked to join—been to Tutwiler and was back. Conner and Linda said they did not approve of Baby Cakes's girl—and that was the end of that.

Recipe of the month: This one Conner was kind enough to share with me. One of her favorites, she said.

First, you get peanuts from the vending machine. Then you get several packets of sugar from the vending machine. Then you add a dab of water and microwave for a few minutes. You take it out and shake—don't stir— the mixture and put it back in to cook a little longer. And there you have it, Big House Brittle.

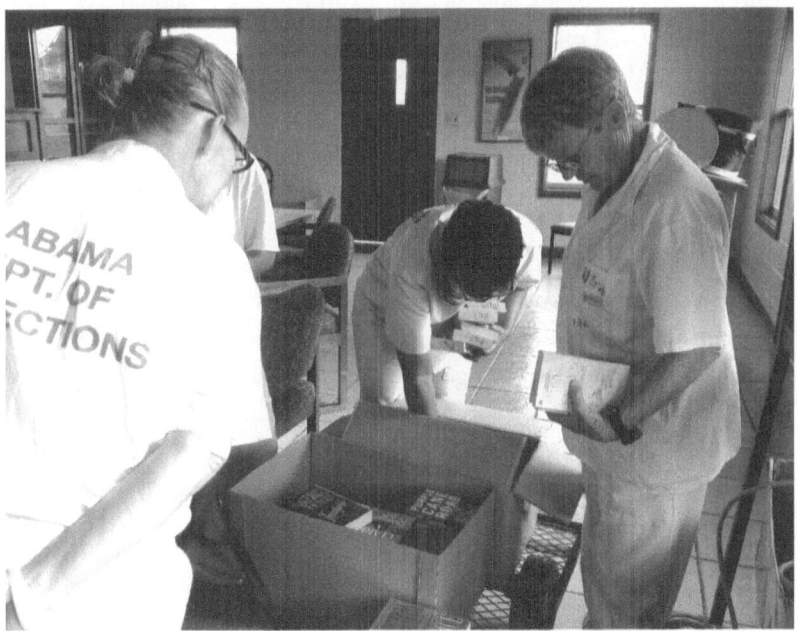

Choosing leisure reads for the month

CHAPTER 9
Betty's Story

We are talking hot—July hot! Thank goodness for the AC in the visitation room. When I hung my car keys up in the check-in office, even in there, with the window unit going full blast, the air was stifling. The supervising guard gave me a quick glance and turned on the PA to announce "Book Club," then waved me on to a waiting Ms. Foley.

Sometimes I think they joined book club because of the refreshments. Other times I believe most of them really do enjoy our monthly reads. But today I know they joined because it's a break from their roasting dorm area and a chance to come into the cool for a couple of hours. As we walked across the grounds pulling our bounty, I noticed a small strip of shade, about four feet wide, being cast by the giant gymnasium-like building that houses everybody. Twenty-five or thirty inmates stood in a single line in the length of its shadow, the only place outside of the living quarters with shade. They were just standing there, lined up like cattle, chatting over shoulders to the person behind or in front of them.

On coming into our space, Linda immediately went over to turn down the temperature on the window unit. As we were pulling tables together to make a common area, a couple of the guards came in and sat for a few minutes under the AC to cool off.

Linda lifted her end of a table that we carried across the room to join to the others. "It's so hot it's hard to sleep at night because of the flies and the heat."

No AC in the dorm, of course, so the big exhaust fans suck in the flies and mosquitoes that seem especially bad this time of year. As we moved tables around and people complained about the heat, Uma came over to me, grinned, and in a soft voice said, "I don't get hot, 'cause I come from Africa." And then, smiling, she walked away.

Conner, the ever-present mother hen: "Y'all remember to wet your T-shirts before you put 'em on. It helps—believe me." Then her mood seemed to suddenly change. She jammed the table she was pushing into some chairs, looked up, shook her head, and slowly began to pull it back again. "Guess I'll be doing this forever—same old, same old, same old."

I looked over to Linda for an explanation. She whispered as the guards were still sitting over in the corner next to the AC. "She didn't get a parole date like she was countin' on."

"You're kidding. I thought, y'all thought, it was a sure thing." I said it too loudly and the others gave me a sharp look. "Well—" I tried to whisper—"y'all said . . ."

"Really, Pat, it ain't over till it's over." Linda pulled a chair up to our group of tables. "And she's taking this one hard. Can't sleep and won't eat." She grabbed another chair and brought it to the tables. "I think she got a five-year setoff." She anticipated my need for clarification. "Means that your parole was not granted and you will get another hearing in five years."

"Five years—yikes! No wonder she's miffed."

Just then Rosalee came bustling in the door, saying she was sorry she was late but she was talking to her new husband on Skype. He was starting a new job and getting his visa and work permit—go figure. Everyone smiled at Rosalee's cheer. In here, we go from one end of the mood spectrum to the other in a matter of seconds.

Linda prattled on. "It's been hot as Hades around here lately and everybody is sick. I haven't gotten my meds in over a week—blood pressure, thyroid, you know—and neither has anybody else."

Recently I had gone on the web to see how long each of my ten had been in prison. Linda has served longer than most—over twenty-three years—and she was originally in for a class C offense. I had asked her why, for a class C, which usually doesn't garner that many years.

"Back at the beginning of my sentence, while I was serving time, I escaped," she said, "and that added to it." Then she walked off to fetch another chair.

"Uh, yeah . . . I guess that'll do it."

In Alabama, felony crimes are divided into three levels: Class A (for which one can be sentenced to no less than 10 years and no more than life or 99 years), Class B (no less than 2 years and no more than 20 years), and Class C (no less than 1 year and no more than 10 years).

I noticed our preparations were slowing to a crawl—the passing-out of food, the positioning of paper plates, the trips to the cooler to get ice for their drinks. I finally realized we were waiting for the guards to get cool enough to leave. As soon as that happened, the mood relaxed. Pammie got up, went over to the AC unit, and pulled out her T-shirt to take double advantage of the wet T-shirt/AC vent combination.

Just as the guards had opened the door to leave, Maya slipped in. She hadn't been to a book club meeting since her daughter had died in the car crash, which was understandable. We all acted as if she had been there all along. She sat quietly during our session, and then, toward the end, she came up to me and whispered in my ear telling me how much she appreciated the condolence card Sara and I had sent her. Then she slipped away.

Seabiscuit sold millions of copies and was on the best-seller list for years, and although I enjoyed it, I thought a story about a horse might not get it with my gang. "Really, Pat—horses?" But, immediately after this read I started corralling used copies of *Unbroken*—another of author Hillenbrand's mega hits.

I was astounded by how much they loved the story of Seabiscuit. Up to this point, no read had ever had such universal appeal for my ten. Most everybody said they had read it. A few had not had time to read the whole thing and wanted to keep their copy to finish up.

As we passed out food, they were already talking about it. That's my measure of a hit—that they are talking about it before we even start eating.

I asked if any of them had ever been near horses before.

Val: "Heck, I used to go to the races in Kentucky all the time with my parents when I was a kid."

Linda: "I used to do rodeo with my family." She caught my quizzical look. "Well, yeah, Pat. I haven't spent my whole life in here, ya know." Immediately she thought better of that . . . "Well, maybe half of it."

I asked how many had ridden a horse at one time or another. Most everybody had. And then I asked what they like most about the story, now that they were aficionados.

Harriettee: "The preface just drew me in and I never stopped after that. She is really an engaging writer."

Conner: "He, Seabiscuit, he was such an underdog. I like it whenever somebody beats the odds."

Ms. Foley: "Yeah, he was the underdog and nobody woulda given him a chance, but he did win and kept on winnin'. One of my favorite stories."

The high point for me was when Uma commented. "Weird to think 'bout what's goin' on in Europe 'round then. Hitler be gettin' ready to start on World War II, and in America we be crazy over a horse."

It's the history teacher in me. I am always thrilled when people relate a particular event to the larger picture of that time. I like to think the book might have broadened some horizons—probably just wishful thinking.

Just then our conversation took its usual right turn.

Seems there was a big influx of meth in here this last month—several of the girls got sky high and were "performing nudeness"—Ms. Foley's quote—in front of the guards. Of course, my women were merely commenting on what had happened with the short-termers. They would never be involved in something that crass—they said.

And speaking of drugs, Betty was back from Tutwiler, having been rehabilitated, I suppose, or because there was no room over there. In any event, I was pleased to be able to give her more of the typed answers to questions about her life that she had left with me a few months back.

This session, Betty spent most of her time sitting quietly, head lowered, looking over her life, typed up neatly in black and white. Once she did look up at me and smile. "Sometimes I couldn't sleep at night, thinking of the questions I wanted to answer."

She's thinner since coming back from Tutwiler, and her skin seems to have taken on a yellowish cast—or maybe it's just my imagination.

I suggested that we take one of the autobiography questions and go around the room so that each person could comment about what they could write, or had written, but only if they wanted to. They seemed amenable.

The question was number 11. *What would you write for your own epitaph?*

Linda's answer was short and to the point. "She can finally rest." (From the one who bustles around all day organizing everyone and everything—

writing letters to me to schedule book times, organizing the library, et cetera.)

Uma: "Mine would be—now don't laugh, Miss Pat—She invented a shot everybody had to take that was to protect you against hate. No one would hate because it would block it out of they brain. No one would judge me cause I'm a felon. Okay, I know this is just wishful thinkin' cause peoples thrive on hate." (From the one who tells all the funny stories and keeps everyone smiling—and incidentally seems to be a drug czar in here. Well, I guess that keeps people happy too—for a time.)

Val: "I was a loving daughter, sister, and friend." (She had been on her way to see about her mother the night she had her wreck that killed a passenger in an oncoming car.)

Betty was the last one who wanted to comment, and the only one who read hers aloud. She flipped to the right page in her typed version, cleared her throat, and began.

> The girl who made mistakes! The woman who suffered for them!

She stopped and looked up at us. "That was all I was gonna write, but I changed my mind." She placed the page flat on the table and began her expanded version, putting into words what so many inmates must feel who are in a similar situation.

> I want the world to know that a long time ago I made a lot of bad decisions and mistakes in my life! But truly I was and still am a good person. I allowed drugs and alcohol to take control of me. Everything in life I ever detested, I became. I was weak to the dope; really weak. Not only did I shatter and destroy my life and my world, plus a lot of others! Randy and Joey [her sons], Mama and Daddy paid dearly, suffered greatly for my wrong doings. The Smith family suffered greatly also. Using drugs does not just affect you, as you think, it affects all who know and love you, plus those who don't.
>
> As this is read, I pray I am in heaven with my mama, husbands, Granny, family & friends! If the Good Lord is willing, I'll send y'all a sign: please never doubt my love, it was real and true! Thank God I finally grew up. Please learn from my mistakes, loved ones. I never want any of you to have to live and suffer the way I did. Maybe I had to go through all of it, so none of you ever would have to. Look for me in a gentle breeze, a funny looking cloud, a flower that just

popped up. Listen for my voice in the wind. I think I'm in heaven and finally at peace. Amen!

We all sat quietly while Betty, moved to tears by her writing, straightened her typed pages and nodded her head slowly.

Harriettee eased up out of her chair and began passing around the tin canister of brownies I had brought for dessert. When she got to me, she whispered, "Fat Jack's Burgers."

High-five—"You got the job. *Congrats.*"

She touched my shoulder and passed to the next person.

Okay, so it's no big deal—a job flipping burgers in a fast food joint, but here in one small room in one overcrowded women's prison out in the boonies south of Montgomery, Alabama, life goes on—successes and failures—this time, for us, a big success.

When it was time to go, the escorting guard, Ms. Foley, and I walked across the grounds toward the exit, Ms. Foley pulling the cart that contained the books left over from our last read, my satchel full of notes, and the empty cardboard boxes that I'll use next time.

Our guard was shuffling along behind, distracted by chatter over his shoulder radio, when Ms. Foley asked, in a whisper, "Do I have to answer the questions you give us to write about our life? Done brought up some bad memories for me."

"No, of course not, Ms. Foley, if you don't want to. It's just an exercise, and speaking of questions, let me ask you one I've been meaning to ask for some time now. When you were sentenced by the court did you—did your lawyer tell you to . . . you did have a lawyer, didn't you?"

"Oh, yeah, I did, but didn't set much store by him. Said I shouldn't go to trial . . . said for me to plead guilty. Said the judge would give me thirty year, but I wouldn't be in maybe five years or so, on account of I'd get years off for good behavior. And here I am, still here."

We paused at the gate to wait for the guard house to buzz us out, and suddenly Ms. Foley was a waterfall of remembrance.

"My daddy, he was the one I most liked. He turned out to be a bad man. And just as I was 'bout to get together with him after years . . . done made him his favorite, coconut cake . . . then he went and got hisself murdered." She rambled on in a cascade of sentences, saying that her cousins had sexually abused her when she was a child and that she had stepbrothers and stepsisters that got better treatment than she ever did. "I was seein' a mind doctor 'bout that time. Doc done give me all sorts of pills for the depression. Why, the night I killed him, he done turned into a monster, big and hairy, right before I up and . . . that's when I done it."

The buzzer sounded, opening the gate. We stepped out into the free world and the telling abruptly stopped as we loaded the leftovers into my trunk.

"Ms. Foley, please don't bring up those bad memories if they make you sad. I never want you to feel that being in the book club is a burden. I would feel terrible if I thought for one minute that anything we did in book club added to your load."

She smiled at me, visibly lightened, as she pulled the cart back toward the chain-link fence.

"One more thing I'm curious about, Ms. Foley."

The guard had gone ahead to open the gate and was holding it for her.

"Did you ever think about filing an appeal—you know, like maybe you weren't in your right mind the night it happened. Do you know what an appeal is?"

She looked at me, remembering back years, standing at the entrance to the barbed wire that had been home for going on two decades now, and then suddenly her head jerked back into the present. "Sure, and I know what appealin' is. Done filed one some years back. Didn't do no good."

Then the gate began to swing closed and she and the guard were gone. While I watched her walk off, I decided that when I had the time, I would try to get a copy of her records and see what really did happen.

Ms. Foley's flowers

CHAPTER 10

Mapping Out Our World

We met earlier this month, as I had needed to be in New Orleans for a meeting during our regular book club time. I have to skip a month every once in a while, or push up the time, but I average about ten or eleven visits a year. Even so, they had read *Life of Pi* and were ready for me.

Winner of the Man Booker. You probably saw the motion picture. Some of mine had even heard of the movie that had been made from the book. And of course, the book had been a best seller to begin with. Sixteen-year-old Pi is immigrating with his family and their zoo animals from India to North America aboard a Japanese cargo ship. Alas, the ship sinks and Pi finds himself aboard a lifeboat with a 450-pound Bengal tiger. Now why can't I think of plots like that?

Everyone said they liked the novel, everyone except Val—so what's new. She said it was too slow and she wasn't into zoos. The others said it did tend to go on and on about zoos at the first, but everyone but Val seemed to have liked it. I had gotten a GradeSaver that had questions in the back and used them as a point of discussion. We briefly talked about the main theme—a belief in God in a broader sense, as Pi incorporated most religious philosophies into his thinking. This did not perhaps sit easily on the shoulders of the more conservative among us—a.k.a. Ms. Foley. However, as a whole the group found it acceptable.

More to our point was discussing the animals in the zoo and the author's theory that they were happier than in the wild because everything was provided for them and they were safe.

"Is that like being in here?" I asked, knowing the ridicule to come. "After all, everything is provided for you. You get your room and board—clothes, three meals a day, medical treatment . . ."

Val, tapping her pencil on the table: "I wouldn't exactly call them meals."

Pammie: "I hadn't had a salad in two years—I'm not kiddin' ya, Miss Pat. You only get fresh greens if you're on work stop—not kiddin' ya."

Conner: "Yeah, I haven't had fresh fruit in a week, much less a salad." She paused, seeing the looks she was getting from the others. "Okay, we did get one apple last week, each person got one—one apple. This place sucks." Conner was still smarting from not getting a parole date and it showed in her whole demeanor—head down, shoulders slumped, as she took her place at the table. She had come in late.

Uma—grinning: "First thing I'm gonna get when I get out—Big Mac and fries."

Ms. Foley: "I could use me some real barbecue."

Me: "Yes, but maybe barbecue and fries aren't good for you. You really would be better off with nourishing food—and the prison administration knows that."

Harriettee knew I was being a smartass, just for the discussion of it. "Listen, Pat, darlin', I can take just as much delight in hardening my arteries as you can." She raised her hand and was about to give me an unseemly gesture but thought better of it.

Me: "But there are some in here that are like that and you know it. They wouldn't eat healthy if you begged them to." I grinned at Harriettee, ready for a zinger from her, but Linda piped up.

"Like who?" Linda said. "Just name one." Her pencil was poised as if to take names and kick butt.

"Well, Darlene what's-her-name, from down in Lowndes County. Ms. Foley has told me about her. She's waaay overweight. And those two in for shoplifting, Shaniqua and Marlana. Baby Cakes was talking about them my last visit. They live out of the vending machines. And what's-her-name, the one that just got back in here a month ago—took the same bunk she had last time."

Perplexed looks at me. "Y'all remember—the one that's been in here since 1980. Linda introduced her to me out in the yard last time we had book club. What a talker that one is. Y'all know, the one with eighteen aliases . . . what's-her-name."

Linda pitched her pencil up in the air and let it drop on her book.

"Really, Pat." Looks of disgust from the others. "They're, most all of them, short-timers—they don't count."

And that was the end of that.

So we proceeded to get out our maps of the world that we use to record the locations of our reads. Each woman began to place a dot on the location of the *Life of Pi* story. Baby Cakes seemed especially interested in the map but placed her sticker in a different part of the ocean than the others. We all like to look at the countries we have visited in our books, but this time Baby Cakes—looking at my map—felt I had placed Pi's boat in the wrong part of the ocean. I tried to explain that the curvature of the earth was such that it was the right place, even though the dot was on the far left and India, where the adventure had started, was on the far right. Of course, I had no—none—nada—credibility.

Then Uma took up the cause and again explained to Baby Cakes that the map was flat and the boat could have ended up where I put it. Then, and only then, was Baby Cakes mollified.

"Sometimes," I smiled at Uma, "I wonder why I even bother to come. I could just as well send in the books and refreshments and let Val record everything—you and Conner and Linda lead the discussion and Harriettee throw in some smarty comments."

Harriettee grinned, reached over, and patted my arm. "We need a note of levity. It brightens our day."

Ms. Foley said quietly, "I like you comin'. You ain't half bad."

"Well, thanks, Ms. Foley."

And all the while, I was secretly delighted that they were taking on these various roles.

Val gave me the list of the paperback books I had brought in so far. By now we must have at least 250 books in here, plus who knows how many romance novels. Too many of those for Val to include in her count. In all fairness to Val, in addition to her other duties, which include cleaning and administrative work, intermittently she serves as a tutor for several hours a week for those who are trying to pass the GED—which is sometimes offered and sometimes not.

A while back I emailed the warden to ask if I could see the library—to get an idea about the capacity. The girls said it was in the hobby room and consisted of three bookcases against one wall, with lots of Christian books—our books and other contributions. And of course, they constantly have to weed out the paperbacks I bring in. The popular ones get trashed in a hurry. In addition, I am told, there is a very small law library off to one side.

The warden never did answer my email, but according to my girls there is not enough room for the bunks, much less books—first things first. I suppose I would rather have a bed than a book . . . I suppose.

Refreshments of the month: Burger Joe's salads, bottled tea, and low-fat fruit yogurt parfait from the new truck stop that has opened up one exit before I get to the prison exit on I-85. Also, homemade brownies that my sister contributed.

All immediately dug in—all except for Maya. She had never really come back to being herself since her daughter was killed in the car accident. She usually sits quietly during discussion, gazing off into other worlds. Always a picky eater, this day she ate from her salad the bacon, cheese, and chicken, then gave the rest of it to the others to divide. I am told that nowadays Maya doesn't eat anything that is green in color.

I had also brought a big bag of candy that I gave to Baby Cakes, thinking she would share—as it was her birthday. She shared, somewhat. I suppose it all depends on what you have in your prison account to spend at the canteen as to how generous you can be.

They are always telling me they don't get fresh greens in here, so I planned to bring salads as the refreshment from now on—some kind of garden salad. I think I have mentioned that Ms. Foley gets a green salad twice a week, when her heart is acting up and she's on work stop, but I am told it consists of lettuce only.

They ate every morsel of the Burger Joe's salads—well, all except for Maya.

One of our individual maps with names of some of the books we read, geographically located

CHAPTER 11
The Alabama Slammers

Tennis event of the day: A few meetings back, I had asked if they would like to join the United States Tennis Association as a member organization, since we had a court—of sorts—and with the membership we would get a tennis magazine at regular intervals. Oh, yes, they were all for it.

Betty said, "Maybe it'll have in there a article 'bout how we can beat up on Ms. Foley in tennis."

Me: "Okay, think of a team name that is appropriate for us and let me know."

This meeting, Harriettee said she and the others had been thinking about it—namely when they were all taking a group shower one day—and they had come up with a couple of names that they would like to offer for my consideration.

"Dandy, what are they?"

"Guilt by Association, or Alabama Slammers."

Harriettee folded her arms and condescended with a smile. "I prefer Guilt by Association. It has a certain legal ambiance, but Conner favors Alabama Slammers."

Ms. Foley: "So do I—Alabama Slammers. Got a ring to it."

Linda: "Yeah, that'll work for me."

Uma: "Ain't half bad."

"Then Alabama Slammers it is." I said I would enroll us with that name the minute I got back home, thinking the magazine and other materials would come to them at the prison. So I did, only to find out later that USTA material couldn't be mailed directly to the prison—posters and materials other than letters are prohibited—so everything addressed to Alabama Slammers now comes to me and I pass it on.

This meeting I presented them with their first copy of *Tennis* magazine that had recently arrived. They were all smiles, passing it around and glancing at the various articles and the mailing label that said Alabama

Slammers. Somehow, we are morphing into a tennis-playing autobiography-writing, book-reading book club.

✳

Hit of the day: One of the occupations to pass time in here is knitting, and over the last month, Conner and Linda and Pammie had knitted not one but four hats for Sara. Really precious, in different colors, and perfect timing because Sara had just had another round of chemo and had shaved off the hair that had not fallen out before. I told them I knew Sara would be thrilled—and she was—and they were all smiles.

I think it must be very gratifying, in their world, to be able to play the role of caregiver to someone on the outside.

Later, when I presented the hats to Sara, she sat down and wrote all the knitters thank-you notes. Additionally, she sent a letter to Betty saying how much she had enjoyed reading Betty's autobiography writing. I had given her copies of the typed version, with Betty's permission of course. Sara didn't have Betty's incarceration number, so she included her note in a letter she sent to Linda. Big mistake—you'll see.

✳

In this age of instant mass communication, every time I connect with the book club, I have to reconfigure my thinking. Think in terms of the days of the old Pony Express that delivered the mail.

Okay, my letter will take three or four days to get there, add a day or two for it to get through inspection and then to be passed around so the others can read it when it does get there, and then their return letter will take another three or four days to get back and then when it does, you often have a screwup, like this letter from Betty to Sara.

> Dear Mrs. Sara,
>
> Hello! I pray this letter finds you doing good and feeling fine!
> Got some bad news! I did not get to receive your letter. The reason is because it was in Conner's envelope. Our letters have to be separate. I did not get to read it or anything! They called Conner to gate 7 to the cruel mail lady and made her tear it up!

Sara

Grrr . . . The woman is just really something serious! It hurt my feelings really bad! But . . . towards her. But I was so excited when Conner told me that you wrote to me. It made me feel very special that you would take the time to drop me a few lines. I am very grateful for that! It would have been a blessing to actually get your letter. That's why it hurt. Because that lady does not know our struggles. What may be going on with us. How desperately we may of needed that particular piece of mail. I've never understood their reasoning the entire time I've been locked up.

I guess I never will.

So . . .

If you do not mind, will you please write to me again!? I am so sorry Mrs. Sara! Also —— is my maiden name. I am in prison under my married name.

I would love to hear back from you. It would mean the world to me. Truly!

Next is the letter Sara had written to Betty, that might have made a difference at that particular time—who knows. Eventually she did receive this one, but by then Betty had been sent back to Tutwiler again for more drug infractions.

Big Canoe, GA

Dear Betty

I read your "MY Life" manuscript and here is what I think:

You are a terrific writer and your own transformation can be an inspiration to others. I am no writer but I am a big reader and let me tell you, I was captivated. Your voice is original authentic, funny and pure. I would have loved the character (you) in those stories even if I didn't know you. Your writing seems to flow easily and naturally to me. Again, I am certainly no expert. This is just one woman's opinion.

You tell such sweet tales of your family and honest stories of your own life experiences. But I wish you would expand on your response to every question because after I finished each one, I wanted to know more. If you ever want me to, I will be glad to write down all the questions that each story triggered for me.

I have no idea how you tie stories together so they become a book but if you just keep writing, maybe that will happen.

Pat said she has some additional pages that you gave her at the last meeting. I can't wait to read them.

And, Betty, I think your experiences can be great lessons to your children. Even if you weren't there when they were growing up, you showed them how people can live with the consequences of poor choices AND YET still transform themselves. Forgive yourself a bit, Betty. You are an amazing woman to have overcome so much and still keep going. All you have is NOW so use it, girl, and I say, WRITE, WRITE, WRITE!

Warm regards, Sara Lindkrantz

(I hope to see you at one of the summer book club meetings. Seems they always fall on the Friday of my chemotherapy appointment)

CHAPTER 12
Conner Gets "The Job"

On our way in, Harriettee met us out in the yard. She was rushing to tell me before she raced across the ground to grab the prison van for work. "I love it at Fat Jack's Burgers. I do everything from working the drive-through window to mopping the floors. And I'm good at it." A quick hug, grinning, and she was gone. Ms. Foley and I looked after her, so pleased, so far.

"Ms. Foley, do you think they pay her anything for working there—as much as they do the regular employees?"

"Don't know, but I do know she's got to pay the prison five dollars a day to ride the prison van to work and back. So you gotta subtract that. There's probably other things they subtract. Hear tell sometimes it adds up to gettin' maybe two dollars a hour."

"Well, I guess that's something—not much but something. Probably the best thing about it is getting out of here for the day."

I could feel additional enthusiasm was in the air the minute I came into the visitation room.

Ms. Foley had said, on the way in, "Conner has a surprise for ya." Big news of the day. Conner had been assigned to work at the governor's mansion. This, for those of you who are not in the know, is the supremo job for long-timers. You get to get out of the prison for the day and go to the governor's mansion (actually next door to the governor's mansion, where the entertainment house is located) and you get paid—not much but you get paid. Those long-timers who don't qualify for regular work out in the community can work here. It's work, but in a government facility—and Conner is one of the few lucky ones. Maybe, just maybe, those in power realized that she was sinking into a deep depression and this might help. In any event, she had been in sixteen years by then and when she was denied parole a few months back after such high hopes, it took a toll. She had begun to lose weight and have a ragged look about her. I was afraid she might turn to the readily available underground medications.

In times past, here's what she had told me her daily schedule had been like, repeated day in and day out, year after year after year—before her big break:

5:00 a.m.—wake up
6:00–7:30—do my state job, which is cleaning up the administration building
8:00—shower, hand-wash clothes
11:30—eat lunch
12:00–2:00—naptime—my favorite time of day
2:00—iron (earn extra money from other inmates for ironing their clothes)
4:00—more of my state job (also, when they are offered, "I participate in any programs from the outside—like book club")
5:00—supper
6:00–10:00—"TV," mail call, miscellaneous
10:00—bed

This day, she walked into our room a new Conner—head back and unabashedly delighted—perhaps the original Conner. I had never seen her without her usual guarded self, shoulders bent slightly forward like a boxer ready to ward off blows. Now when she stepped in, shoulders back and smiling, everybody clapped. She rushed over and slapped me on the shoulder, bubbling over with a new light that must have been hidden away all this time. Amid a profusion of babble about how she was going to love it at the "gov's palace," she immediately said she couldn't stay. She had to go, and just wanted to tell me about her new job—and then she was through the door, leaving us all mellowed out and smiling.

We will miss her and her organizing ways, but I couldn't be happier for her. She told us she would be able to visit from time to time when her work schedule permits, so "whatever you do, don't take me outta the book club."

✳

Before we moved on to the book of the month, I asked Linda to tell us about *Wide as the Waters*, by Benson Bobrick. It's about the translation of the English Bible. I had been looking for a paperback copy and brought it to her last month. It's so hard to find a read that everyone likes that when a member has a particular interest, I try to accommodate. (Linda: biblical history—Uma: history of her African American forebears—etc.) From Linda's account, I could tell she had read it and seemed to enjoy it. Although not very interested, the rest of the book club listened politely for the short time it took to hear her report.

On to the book of the month—*I Know Why the Caged Bird Sings*, by Maya Angelou. I don't think to myself, Okay, we've had several books by white authors and so now we'll have a book by a Black author—nonsense. I try to get the best I can find at the time. Sara had seen three or four of these in paperback as she was collecting free used paperbacks from a contributing library in her part of North Georgia, and then I ordered the rest online from a used books dealer. When I have free finds like this classic, I feel like I've unearthed real treasure.

Once again, we were trying out the idea of a couple of the women being responsible for reporting on the read each month: this time Rosalee, our newlywed, and a new member, Keisha. Keisha was new to me, but she'd been around the circuit of the women's facilities for years, Tutwiler, then Louisiana, then Birmingham, and now here. (Don't ask me how the system works. I long ago stopped trying to fathom the Alabama Department of Corrections. It is a miracle that it works at all—short staffed and no money and so many prisoners that they are stuffed in every nook and cranny. Have I said that before?)

Whereas Keisha was completely new to our group, I could see why the girls chose her—very cool customer—a persona that says she can handle, and has handled, anything that might come her way. Back in the day, most everyone else in our group took a plea bargain before they ended up in here—and were eventually sorry they had. Not Keisha. The others tell me she went to trial and then was found guilty by a jury—her badge of honor. In here that's like saying, "I skipped college and went straight for my PhD.

Don't mess with me. I know the ropes." In our group she was given elbow room from the get-go.

Now that Conner was off doing chores for the governor and wouldn't be here most of the time, Linda had made a seamless transition from librarian to group leader. All seemed satisfied with the change. I nodded to Keisha and Rosalee to begin their reports.

The two of them led the discussion by asking questions—kind of a haphazard job, but they did have questions prepared for the first half of the book, and most of the others knew the answers.

At this point Pammie, sitting down at the end of the table with Baby Cakes and Maya, decided to give us her take on the inadequacies of our book club. "Ya see, Ms. Pat. The problem is this—if you don't mind me saying so."

Having stepped out on a conversational limb, which was unlike Pammie, she continued: "By the time we come back to group meeting every month, we've read the assigned book two or three weeks ago and we forget. That's why we don't know the answers to some of the questions . . . Sometimes."

I countered with, "Well, maybe you should wait until a week before we meet and then read it."

"Something might interfere and then we wouldn't get it done at all." Pammie grinned at me, knowing she didn't believe that any more than I did. I am still a novice and always will be to the ways of prison life, but I do feel I should at least make an attempt to question them once in a while.

"Like what?" I said. "What might interfere with your reading it a few days before our scheduled meet?"

"Well, something." Now Pammie had both elbows on the table and her chin cradled in palms.

I never insist that book club members read a book. Ms. Foley is a case in point. If it makes them feel uneasy or brings back bad memories it doesn't serve its purpose. Pammie has been in the system many, many years and will finish up her sentence one of these days. Her strategy—it seems to me—is to chill as best she can until that time. She's not even trying for parole. That means smoking marijuana when she wants to—not an offense that will get you sent back to Tutwiler—but never the hard stuff, which will. That way Pammie goes along to get along.

"Well, what?" I asked again. "What's your assigned daily job in here, that takes up so much of your time?" The others began to snicker, knowing what was coming.

Real Job assignment (like Harriettee had in the kitchen when she first came here) in a facility that is way overcrowded to begin with is rare, at best. In our group, outside of Librarian Linda, Val, who keeps a running list of our books and who works in the administrative office, and Ms. Foley, who keeps the grounds, there is not that much left in the way of something to occupy your time—trash collector, runner for the office, working in the laundry when needed, and similar chores.

"So what is it?" By now, I was curious myself. "What is your day job in here?"

Pammie sighed. "Number 3—wiping it down."

And of course, I had to ask. "What's that mean? Is that a code for something that you do . . . number 3?"

The others grinned at each other, waiting for the punch line.

Linda: "It means, Pat, that she wipes down table number 3 in the recreation room every day. That's her job."

Me: "That's her work? That's her whole work load?"

Now I felt like I may have insulted Pammie but she pantomimed wiping the table and grinned. "Hell of a lot of work."

Uma: "And a great job she does too . . . with her wiping cloth. Ain't never seen it done better." Uma leaned back in her chair. "Just wipes that table clean as a whistle every single day. Takes what—all of twenty seconds?"

Linda: "Well, she probably has to do it three or four times a day."

Uma: "Okay, a total of a minute and a half."

Me: "That's all you do—that's all?"

Pammie: "Well . . . I have to wash out the cloth once in a while."

※

After Keisha and Rosalee had finished their part of the program, we went around the table, for those who wanted to add additional comments about *Caged Bird*, but not before Keisha concluded: "I didn't like the book per se, but I'm a huge fan of her poems." That in itself drew a roll of the eyes from Uma, as she does not like to hear Black members criticize Black authors—but then again, Keisha is the exception.

A thought—precipitated by Keisha's mention of poems. One of these days, I must bring a book of poems as book of the month.

We continued with Pammie's take on the read. "I didn't like the book 'cause of the way they done the kids. I didn't like the way they done the blacks back in the fifties either. . . . Just my thinkin'." The voice barely above a whisper now, head down staring at the table. "Probably others mightn't think so."

Uma, obviously feeling very intellectual on this day: "I loved the book. It was very extra and deep, yet it was evasive and didn't tell the whole story of the situation."

Me: "Uh . . . I didn't quite get that, Uma."

Uma—insulted. "Plain as the nose on your face, Miss Pat."

At which point I began to verbally backpedal: "Well, I'll go back and reread . . . uh . . . parts of the story." Even though I didn't know what in the world she was talking about—"very extra"?—I would never want to belittle somebody else's understanding—if that's what it was . . . or maybe it was Uma's usual bs. The main point of this book club is to read the book. Keep saying that to yourself, Pat.

Val was more down-to-earth: "I didn't like where she was raped and then her mother and grandmama didn't wanna talk to her about it. She had to deal with it on her own." Maybe Val had read the book of the month after all. I shouldn't be such a skeptic.

Ms. Foley: "The book was good to me especially 'cause of it bein' a true story, but on a scale of 1 to 10, I'd say a 6—but I did read it and I usually don't . . . read that kinda book."

Refreshments: Burger Joe's salads, fruit parfait, and my sister had altered her contribution this time with apricot squares that all devoured. Apple cider for a drink, because fall was in the air. And paper cups for the apple cider with the Auburn football logo on the sides—'cause football is in the air.

Without Conner, we had an extra salad. I suggested we give it to one of the guards. "Never hurts to get in a few brownie points."

"No way"—practically in unison. Seems the guards always get first dibs and take all the good stuff anyway. They proceeded to tell me about an event sponsored by one of the churches a few months back, in which there was a choice of barbecue or chicken and the guards tried to take all the barbecue when it was meant for the inmates.

So we divided what was left among ourselves. The girls divvied up the salad. I ate the yogurt fruit parfait.

As we sat eating our dessert, Rosalee, who was for once in a talkative mood, began to tell us more about how she had originally come in contact with her new husband. It seems that he had seen her on a TV documentary in the UK (we TV—*Women Behind Bars*). It was then that he started corresponding with her. She said that she felt meeting him had saved her life, as she had been very depressed before they met. Recently, she had been back to the court where she was arrested. She said back then her case was so obviously mishandled and now, thanks to her new husband—and his knowledge of the U.S. criminal system—she now knows parts of the criminal code by heart, reciting numbers and paragraphs to us. Love works in mysterious ways?—I guess.

The latest rumor: Once again, my group is excited, thinking they will get out soon because of this new initiative that has been presented to the Alabama legislature to reform the prison system and cut down on the overpopulation. Maybe the Feds will come in and take over the whole system if something isn't done soon. Or maybe they will see how much things need improving and just go on and let everybody out and they can all go home.

Yeah, right.

Drink of the month: hand sanitizer punch. One of the short-timers tried it last month, and my girls stood around and watched the result.

Seems you take a big container of hand sanitizer and add enough salt to make the gel go to the bottom and the alcohol come to the top and—according to them—get ready to be really, really, really sick. Uma said the girl who did it said she was so sick she thought she was gonna flat-out die.

Well, I guess so. At some point along the way, "flat-out dyin'" would probably have been preferable.

CHAPTER 13

Ms. Foley Falls for Harry

November, and the weather has turned cooler, not cold yet, but it seems more tolerable. For some time now Val and Linda had been asking if we might read one of the *Harry Potter* books. Most of the others had not heard of *Harry Potter,* or cared that the novels were all the rage for younger readers. I decided to get as many different *Harry Potter* titles as I could round up and have the girls pass them around. Some were a little dubious about so many books. So we decided to give ourselves two months to read them all.

I had found copies of seven of the novels in paperback, in various stages of wear.

In the end, the read varied. They either read all seven, or some or none. Ms. Foley all seven—Val none.

The day of our November meeting, Ms. Foley came in late. When Sara and I drove up to the prison, I had seen her out on the mower, cutting grass. Harriettee had done the honors with the cart at the gate, as she had a day off from her town job. She followed my gaze. "It's not so hot today, but she's the oldest one in book club and sometimes she's out there on days when it was 101 in the shade."

Later Ms. Foley came in dirty and messy. "Don't touch me"—and we didn't. She sat down and began eating her salad. "I ain't got so much pleasure out of a book in a long time as I done them *Harry Potter* books. So funny."

Harriettee smiled at her and looked over to me. "You should see her. She comes to get another one out from under my bed, sometimes in the middle of the night." Harriettee is the designated keeper of all the *Harry Potter* books. They're in her box under her bunk. "I see her sometimes at night, sneaking over to my bunk and rummaging through to get another one to read at first light."

The others had enjoyed *Harry Potter,* but not to the degree of Ms. Foley. "I loved all of them books. They was sooo funny." She had obviously seen the books in an entirely different light than most. (I am thinking of half of the twelve-year-olds in the country, who see it as high adventure.) She stopped between bites, long enough for a critique—"He wasn't evil, or a partner of the Devil, like some in my church done told me he was." She fished around in her salad looking for a small tomato, her favorite. "Some of my church people, ya know, they ain't havin' none of *Harry Potter* and I don't see why, now that I done read all them books."

That alone was worth the read. Knowledge in little bits and pieces.

Sara had come with a gift. She brought us all bookmarks she had designed especially for our book group. Her version depicts The Patron Saint of Books on one side with the formal name of our book club—The Seekers— and on the reverse, crossed tennis rackets and our tennis name—Alabama Slammers. My group is always so pleased to get anything that is within code and distinguishes them from the short . . . well, you know.

And speaking of tennis and short-timers. I was told that the short-timers were once again messing up the tennis rackets and that we needed more that would be designated for book club members only. Seems that Ms. Foley was on work stop for a while and couldn't play tennis. Now— somehow—she has been taken off work stop and is a tennis-playing fool again.

Linda: "Every time I look out there to our court, Granny Foley is play-ing, morning and night."

Me: "Who, among y'all, plays with her?"

Uma: "Are you kiddin'? She be wearin' all us out and then she even keep on playin'—even play with the burned brains—and we ain't got a shortage of them 'round here."

"Can't keep up with her." Betty gave Ms. Foley's shoulder a slight punch. "Almost broke a ankle tryin' to run down one of her balls the other day."

Ms. Foley grinned and accepted the accolades. "Nobody beats up on me in the tennis. See?" She pointed to her knees. "These here are the pads I was tellin' you 'bout. Made a pair for me and one for Pammie, 'cause Pammie fell on the court the other day."

They were bright colored knitted pads with strings in the back to tie them on and pockets sown in the front. For cushioning, Ms. Foley had knitted the pockets to fit Kotex pads. She and Pammie looked delighted with Ms. Foley's invention. "Now when I fall on the court, don't hurt half as bad."

I had gotten permission, and we went out to the court to watch my ten play. Sure enough, Ms. Foley was the colossus everyone else said she was. She wasn't the picture of great tennis form—far from it—but she was the picture of persistence. Just gets the ball back, and back, and back.

"So, what kind of scoring do y'all use?" I hadn't quite understood the way they were determining the winner, only that every time, Ms. Foley seemed to win.

"What?"

We hadn't had a chance to talk about scoring yet, and I was curious as I hadn't quite followed their method. "How do y'all decide who's won? Explain to me the method you use—to see who wins. I know Conner had said, at one time, that she could teach basic tennis to y'all, but since she's working now . . ."

They looked at me like I wasn't too bright.

"Well, Pat, it's the last man standing. You go out and see if you can beat Ms. Foley. You hit the ball till she hits it past you and then you sit down and the next person tries to beat her."

"Have you ever thought about maybe no-add scoring? You know, play to four points and then get a winner?"

"Why would we want to do that? That would take all day. Really, Pat."

Silly me. It seems our games in here would be geared to our lifestyle and the size of our court—as I suppose it should be.

※

And a surprise. As I left this time, I was told I couldn't come back unless I had my PREA certification.

"My what?" Suddenly PREA is all the rage in here, but I had heard nothing about having to be qualified before I could enter. It seems that the Prison Rape Elimination Act (PREA) that was signed into federal law way back in 2003 during the Bush administration is now—years later—to be enforced in here. All the inmates and any people associated with them—people like me—must be schooled in this law. That means everyone must take a course to learn about what their responsibilities are and how they should act to prevent rape and their legal responsibility to report it—if it happens. As I understand it, the inmate schooling goes something like this. They are shown a video about rape reporting and rape prevention. Then the warden talks as part of the training. Then there is more discussion. Then everyone is certified.

All volunteers are expected to get the same schooling. After that, everyone's given a card that shows they have completed the course—prisoners and guards and all those who come in contact with the prison population. It's a new push to keep inmates from getting pregnant and to prevent their being taken advantage of. Probably caused by all the improprieties going on in our sister facility Tutwiler. I had recently read an article about a three-year-old little boy being raised by relatives—a result of the mother's rape in prison. (Remember, reader—no matter how consensual it might have been—like Conner had told us early on—it is always considered rape because the guard holds the power.)

It has garnered some good results so far. Now the showers in here have curtains so the guards can't stare at the inmates as they take showers, and the toilets are more private than before. Now the inmates must change clothes in the bathroom and not out in the bunk area. I don't see how they have room to change in the bunk area anyway, but what do I know. Now they say the male guards—in dread of losing their jobs and their pensions—won't go anyplace unless they go together, for fear of being accused of some impropriety—all of this, much to the delight of my gang.

As a result of this adherence to the letter of the law, I was barred from coming to book club for a month or two, until I got my PREA designation. I hadn't had time to attend one of the classes that were offered to volunteers in Montgomery as I live in a different part of Alabama, and some of the time in Atlanta. So I turned to accountant Val, whom I have decided must run the place. She in turn talked to one of the lieutenants and got her phone number for me. I called the lieutenant and she said she would certify me when I came for the next meeting.

So, next meeting, I went in with all my goodies—salads from Burger Joe's, parfaits, extra paperbacks, Girl Scout cookies, brownies, old magazines. The lieutenant came in with the certification paper Sara and I had already signed months ago and said for us to watch a video as we set up for the club. As Val and Linda pulled up tables and unpacked food, we watched the video, which says, basically, you are liable if you don't report abuse. All-righty, then. And with that we were certified.

Val was dismissive of the whole thing. "In this place, some of the inmates have been known to make false accusations against some of the guards—or false accusations against their fellow inmates—if they're jealous of 'em or they're jealous of a relationship they're having with a guard. So what's new about a PREA card?" She paused a minute to think about it. "But then again sometimes it's true, like last week, I heard a guard was caught, in the act, with another inmate at Tutwiler." She turned to me and shrugged her shoulders. "See. Ya never know."

Ms. Foley added, "PREA card ain't nothin' but a piece of paper. It ain't true half the time they report it. Don't make no never-mind. If people wanna do bad, they gonna do bad."

I suppose in a place that is full of people who are trained in unconventional survival methods—not to mention the burned brains among us—this he-said-she-said is to be expected. Perhaps a microcosm of the larger world—just less subtle?

"How in the world did you know all that stuff that goes on at Tutwiler?" I ask Val.

"Well, Pat, it's like this . . ."

"Never mind. Never mind. Don't tell me." I started walking toward the visitation center. "I don't want to know. I got my PREA card and that's that."

What have things come to when I am going to all sorts of lengths to get certified so I can get back in here?

STAFF FIRST RESPONDER DUTIES

Upon learning of an allegation of a PREA related incident, the first responder staff shall:

1) Ensure that the victim (s), aggressor(s), and witness are physically separated;

2) Protect and preserve the crime scene until appropriate steps can be taken to collect evidence;

3) Request that the victim not bathe, wash, brush teeth, eat, drink, smoke urinate or defecate;

4) Ensure that the alleged abuser no bathe, wash, brush teeth, eat, drink, smoke, urinate or defecate;

5) If the first responder staff is not security staff, the responder should request the alleged victim not take any actions that would destroy evidence notify a security staff.

6) Do not show the alleged victim (s aggressor(s), or witness any evidence, such as, but limited to, pictures or video footage of the incident, and do not interview any of these parties on the specifics of the incident.

7) As soon as possible first responders shall notify the Shift Commander of the incident and draft and ADOC Form 302-A, Incident Report.

My PREA card

CHAPTER 14

A New Warden . . . for Five Months

"God, you got in—and with food." Uma was staring at the salads like they were from outer space, lifting the see-through containers out of their plastic bags, holding them up to make sure there was real food in them. "How'd you do that?" The others came straggling in, some with wet hair, lucky to get a shower when the water was hot. Others were pulling on shirts and buttoning them up.

Uma, still amazed: "We didn't expect you—and with food."

"I just walked in like I usually do and gave my keys and driver's license like always. What's the big deal? What's going on?" I had noticed that Ms. Foley was not sitting in her usual place out on the grounds when I pulled up to park and she had murmured, in front of the guard, something about not expecting me, but I had thought it was because she had other duties to perform—maybe cutting more grass—whatever.

"Pat, you never keep up." Linda was shaking her head, eyes to the ceiling. "The warden, remember him, our warden? He's been moved to another facility, like a month ago, right after you left last time."

"And so? What's new about that? Wardens are always shuffling around, aren't they?"

"And so," Linda looked around to the others, "there's a *woman* in charge in here now and she's . . . how shall I say this nicely? She's a b—"

"Don't say it. You know Miss Pat don't cotton to that kinda talk."

"It rhymes with witch. That's as nice as you can get." Uma began placing plastic-covered salads at each place, along with napkins and plastic utensils.

Linda was unscrewing bottled tea I had bought at the truck stop.

"So, what's so terrible about her? She's a woman—I thought that would be a point in her favor."

Linda was lining up glasses to pour the tea. "She does things all different. We were used to our old warden. Just last week, one of the inmates in here, she got a urine test and she tested positive for marijuana and guess what?"

"I can't imagine—what?" I had begun to unload books.

"She was sent back to Tutwiler, that's what." She nodded to the others and they nodded back.

"Sent back? Just for marijuana?" I sat down hard in the chair by Ms. Foley. "Yikes. Nobody in here gets sent back to Tutwiler just for smoking marijuana—only the hard stuff. Doesn't she know that? What is she thinking?" I was as amazed as the others. "The new warden needs to get adjusted to our way of doing things around here." I caught the others looking at me in an odd way and realized . . . My Lord, Pat, what are you saying? Have you gotten so adjusted to the malfeasance in here that you are beginning to adopt their value system? I coughed feebly and lowered my head, pretending to look for something in my book satchel. "Well, I'm just saying . . ."

Pammie: "Yeah, well . . . listen to this. We been havin' bed checks in the middle of the night—two times a night, turning on the lights and waking everybody up. You can't get no sleep. And Rosalee, ya don't see her here, do ya? She asked for a transfer up to Birmingham—couldn't get no sleep—and she got it. Left to go up there as soon as she could."

"Rosalee, our bride? You're kidding. She's in Birmingham now and so quick? Usually it takes months. That new husband of hers must really know the ropes."

I sighed, remembering that in years past, the place to be in the women's prison system in Alabama was here. Inmates would ask to be transferred here, remembering the old nickname, the Country Club of Alabama's Women's Prisons. Long-gone days.

Ms. Foley: "And the church group tried to bring in food last week and they wasn't allowed to—new rules all over the place."

Linda: "And that new tennis lining equipment you were gonna bring us to repaint the lines so we can see them again? Forget about it. No tennis around here now."

"*What?* Everybody loves tennis. It's the one thing you can go out and play any time. And it's so healthy. Ms. Foley—what'll she do . . . and all y'all . . . ?" I caught myself, not wanting to be the one to trash the new administration right off the bat. "Well, now . . . maybe it's just temporary."

Linda: "Could be, but nobody knows anything right now. They say this new one will be here for five months and then she's gonna retire. I'm hoping so."

※

After we had settled into our salads, and everyone was satisfied they were real, I turned the talk to the book of the month.

After my experience with the *Seabiscuit* read, I had finally corralled enough paperbacks to make this one a book club read. Another Laura Hillenbrand blockbuster—*Unbroken*. The story of a heroic World War II solider. Since it was a rather long book, I had given everyone two months to read it, but it was kind of like what happened with *Poisonwood Bible*. Everyone scarfed this one up like melting ice cream—scared to let it go, so enthralled were they.

Ms. Foley: "That book you brought us, Miss Pat? I just can't believe what a human body can stand."

Pammie, pouring ranch dressing all over her Burger Joe's salad and squeezing the remainder in the plastic packet straight into her mouth, stopped just long enough to add: "That *Unbroken* book is the best book I ever read and that Louie is the toughest man of the war—and he had a heart to help others survive. Amazin' to me."

And when you talk about enduring pain, Pammie must know its meaning. She had told us earlier—"Sometimes I feel like I been in here since I was a little child."

She says she doesn't remember—since she almost died herself in the wreck—face all cut up, teeth knocked out or close to it, nose broken. "I don't remember what happened." (Where have I heard that before?) Pammie is another one who took a plea bargain and was sorry. More than likely she will be here until she is let out—EOS—if she is ever let out.

Linda was passing out brownies, placing each one on a napkin and then dividing the two or three remaining pieces into equally minuscule squares to give out again.

I said, "So, what did you think, Linda—about the book?" She stopped mid-slice to consider.

"How somebody can withstand anything put before them and survive like that." She began slicing again. "Best written book I've seen."

I turned to Maya, who was sitting up ramrod straight in her corner chair, out of the way. She put down her plastic Burger Joe's knife—as she had been separating each ingredient in her salad into different piles—and cleared her throat. "*Unbroken* was a highly emotional page-turning book that I enjoyed very much."

Now that she had decided to say something, I was hoping for more, but . . .

Uma interrupted. "Don't give me none of that. It was great! When you know what somebody else can take, it makes you not give up so quick!" Uma, grinning and taking a big slug of tea: "My kinda story."

Pammie sat back, having scarfed down her salad, and now she was chilling out on brownies. "If you don't mind me saying so, what I liked about the book is how Louie stayed alive. The things he went through in the ocean and in the POW camp." This from the one whose main goal is to stay out of everyone's way—finish up her sentence and go home.

And Keisha, the no-plea-bargain dean. "*Unbroken* was the best history book I have ever encountered. The part that touched me the most was when Louie met Bill Graham and he let go of his past and gave his life to Christ."

"I was amazed at how resilient they all were and what he went through and survived. This book wasn't exactly my favorite, but close." Guess who? Val, our accountant.

Along the way, others had confided to me what I had suspected, that Val is so discerning because she doesn't read all of the book of the month most of the time—and therefore criticism is an easy out. Ain't it universal.

All in all, I think they like the fact that somebody was worse off—a lot worse off—than they are and had survived. A huge success.

This time, after we had finished eating and were discussing *Unbroken*, I was the one who veered the subject off-track. "So, what about this new plan that I'm hearing about that the governor is touting—wants to build a series of new prisons, tearing down the old ones and putting up new ones, literally changing the face of the Department of Corrections? Fantastic, huh?"

I was sure my comments would elicit some sort of new and creative plan for getting out early or changing their status.

I got nothing. Like they had heard it a million times before, which, of course, they had. Not one eyebrow was raised.

Uma: "Politics as usual."

Linda: "Why, Uma, what makes you think for one minute they are not gonna tear down all the old prisons and build new ones?"

Even after several weeks, the enthusiasm for this particular book bled over into this part of a letter from one of the girls to Sara. She hadn't been able to attend the last meeting, and they like to keep her in the know.

> Hi Sara,
> We all made Pat proud by reading the book. Because some of the girls just wouldn't read the books she chose. We read Laura Hillenbrand's "Unbroken." It was so good. Pat asked us to stop at chapter 21 but we couldn't put it down. So Great!
> Stay strong and continue to get healthier. We would like to be able to see you again soon. Cooler weather is on the way.
> And I can't wait!
>
> Take care—
> Always, ——

CHAPTER 15

Betty—Back to Tutwiler—
Again, and Again, and Again

Ms. Foley was in fine fettle. She and her helpers had just finished weeding her beautiful flowerbeds that run along the walkways. The flower seeds the church ladies brought did exceptionally well this year, but what do I know. I think I'm successful if I harvest one tomato per vine—that is, if I get crazy and plant a vine.

Ms. Foley was still a little dirt stained but ready with the cart when I arrived.

As we were walking back across the yard, Conner came rushing up to me and gave me a hug. I was surprised but delighted to see her.

"How are things at the governor's mansion? Things working out okay? How do you like it? Are you working your fingers to the bone or is it a cinch? Tell, tell."

She was brimming with news. "Great, just great. I love working over there. So interesting. They have one of your books in the library with all the Alabama authors. Saw you coming in and I had to come say hello. I'm on my way to catch the van over there—crazy schedule today. Maybe I can come and visit book club next time—or one of these times."

"Sure, come on. One of the girls said you were thinking of getting out of the book club—now that you're working."

The eyes immediately narrowed. "Who told you that? Whoever it was, don't listen to them. I have no idea of getting out of the book club—gotta run." She gave me another quick hug and turned to go. "So much to tell you . . ." And she was off, sprinting across the yard toward the work van, but not before she turned one last time and called, "Tell Sara hello."

"She looks great." I watched her off in the distance, running up to the gate, waiting to board the van and head out.

Ms. Foley was all smiles. "She ain't the same person she was. That place done saved her."

Me: "Looks like it. I'll bet she's dusted every book in the library and washed every window to a sparkle."

"Probably." Ms. Foley pushed the cart forward. The guard and I followed.

※

Although different members had been giving me their journal questions to be transcribed by my sister Joanne, we had not, for some time now, carved out space during book club to talk about their individual efforts at writing their life stories. I was rather dubious about our group keeping on course without a book to center us, but then again, when has a book ever kept us centered?

In our meeting place, after setup, I handed out four or five more composition books (a dollar each at Dollar Tree) to some who said they had already filled up the first one. I was so pleased that they seemed to be taking great interest in answering the autobiography questions. Perhaps a cause for reflections, or if nothing else, a wonderful journal to show their friends and family—if and when. Most, by the way, have lovely cursive handwriting. I suppose cursive is becoming a thing of the past, but this group learned it well.

From time to time different groups will come into the prison and hold a series of classes. Recently one of the car companies here in the state held a series of classes in the prison geared to explain about working in the automobile industry—if and when. Everyone was tested at the end, and my gang said that the older inmates like themselves scored higher than the younger ones. Of course, they were delighted. The general consensus among my posse seems to be that the younger generation is not as grounded in the fundamentals as in the past—at least in here they aren't. Their handwriting is barely legible. Some write in print only.

※

Now, having finished our salads, we started around the room to share answers to some of the autobiography questions.

Question 1: What would you do if you had all the money in the world and could do anything you wanted to?

Uma: "If I could do anything, I'd travel and explore."

Harriettee (who had the day off from Fat Jack's Burgers and had joined us): "I'd make sure all children were loved and cared for that come into this world."

"Wait a minute, where's Betty?" I hadn't noticed she was missing. The autobiography questions had reminded me of Betty and her heartfelt answer the last time we talked autobiography, some months back. (Remember? What would you want as your epitaph?)

Linda stopped dividing brownies long enough to look up: "She's back in Tutwiler."

"Again? Damn. What happened this time . . . as if I don't know."

Ms. Foley was starting on her share of brownie. "Whatcha s'pect? I done told ya last time you come. She was hangin' out in the corner with them druggies soon as she got back from Tutwiler last time. You go over in that corner and you'll smell like marijuana the whole day long."

Keisha nodded. "She copped some drugs from a prisoner who was about to get out, EOS, and when that girl was leaving, she gave up all the people she had sold to and guess who one of them was?" She said, "It happens." And then she thought better of that. "It doesn't happen to *me*. I don't do that sort of thing. But it does happen."

"Darn, and I had more of her autobiography answers to give her." When my sister typed them up, she had commented that Betty seemed a natural with her writing—overly dramatic perhaps, but interesting reading.

Keisha: "Keep them. She'll be back."

I was perturbed because I liked Betty and she seems so devoted to her boys that she wants to get back to, one of these days—but at the same time so vulnerable. "I don't understand why y'all couldn't try to help her—keep her away from that kind of thing. You might have some influence on her."

I got jaded looks. I said, "Well, you might."

Linda: "Forget it, Pat—she's a big girl and it was her responsibility. We got problems enough of our own."

Uma: "Besides, she already done passed four drug tests 'fore she finally got caught this time." Grinning and taking a sip of tea. "Some kinda record, if you ask me."

"Okay, okay, I guess y'all are right. Back to the questions. You were saying, Harriettee?"

"Yeah, Harriettee," Uma said. "Tell Miss Pat 'bout the reunion you done had with your family last week."

"I meant the autobiography quest—"

"Can you believe it, Pat?" Immediately Harriettee sat up straight, all smiles. "My kids—I hadn't seen them since they were little, they came to visit, with my mom. My girls are sixteen and twenty-one now. We had such a nice visit. Talked about everything under the sun."

She leaned toward me and pulled up her sleeve. "And I showed them my arms, and look, hardly any scarring now."

Everyone nodded approval.

"And my mother said, 'I hope you'll not be tempted when you get out.'"

Snickers and knowing chuckles from everyone.

Linda: "Like this place is so pristine."

Harriettee: "I told Mom, I can get it in here whenever I want, and I haven't been tempted—so not to worry."

She rubbed her clean arm. "They said I looked great."

Ms. Foley: "And you do, honey."

Harriettee, explaining the whole thing away: "You know, my uncle, and I think my grandparents, they were alcoholics."

She sat back, in the glow of it all—contemplating her past. "My girls and my mother had been writing me a lot before they came. Guess they didn't want to come all this way from out West if it wasn't true." She looked at me and shrugged. "Got hooked when I started taking pain meds after my cesarean. Honestly, I just liked the feeling from the beginning. After that, I went out on the street and bought it—went straight to shooting up heroin. Pretty soon I had to have it just to be able to go to work and teach school, and carry on a normal life, otherwise I was too sick."

I was sitting there looking at somebody who had been completely re-born—physically and mentally—and in a prison where drugs were readily available. At least it looked that way to my untrained eye. The mystery of the ages—how some can get off and others seem doomed. There is a SAP (Substance Abuse Program) for all incoming inmates who have drug-related sentences, but it doesn't seem to make a dent.

Val piped up, waving a piece of paper. "If we want to keep getting books we like, y'all need to sign this card." She was holding a notecard. Sara had made several of them for us to use on occasions like this. She is such an artist that she can make greeting cards, bookmarks, anything we might need.

And I had been falling right into the wandering conversation—forgetting the agenda, of course. "One of the libraries up in Pickens County, Georgia, let Sara go in and pick out a bunch of old paperbacks she knew y'all would like, and we need to thank them."

Val handed it off and the card began its trip around the room. "Get busy, girls."

Pammie looked up from her card signing, pausing to contemplate. "What am I gonna do if one of these days, I finally do get out of here? I don't get but ten dollars and a goodbye. Where would I get a job? What would I do? I don't know how to do nothin'. Even if I was to go to a half-way house, after a month or two, you gotta start payin' rent."

And I said, "Oh, you'll find something," knowing perfectly well that it would be a hard slog—with a prison record—without much of an education—and no particular skills to fall back on. Sometimes, Pat, you can be so trite—and at exactly the wrong moment.

"Problem is," Val said, "Pammie has lots of marks on her record for smoking marijuana—not enough to get sent back to Tutwiler but enough to keep her from getting parole."

And I asked the usual novice question: "What about family?"

Pammie, with a half smile. I couldn't tell if she was joking or putting me on. "All of my family is in jail—or they won't talk to me."

"Do you ever have any visitors? Maybe you could ask them about some job prospects when you get out."

"Don't have no visitors."

"I don't either," Linda said. "Have any family that'll talk to me, right now anyway."

Val: "Has it ever occurred to you, Pat? Maybe some people in here don't want to get out. Not any of us, of course, but for some, being in here is the first time they've ever had any sense of belonging, like chubby Franny what's-her-name, the one with the eighteen aliases—the one we talked about a few months back. She told me one time that all the people she knew were in here. Maybe the thought of being thrown out into the wide world with no backup is terrifying. If I had no family, no friends, and I was put out on the sidewalk with a bag of my belongings and ten dollars, what would I do?"

As I was contemplating this completely useless question, Ms. Foley got up to leave.

"Are you okay, Ms. Foley?" I was concerned that our conversation had brought up some bad memories.

"Oh, yeah. I'm fine. Just gotta go. Warden wants me to dig up some of my flowers that she likes so she can take 'em home to her place to have after she's gone. She usually leaves out pretty soon in the afternoon, so I don't wanna miss her. Ya know she's gonna retire soon."

"I had heard that."

After a short time on the job, our present warden would be retiring in a few more months—and I took it no tears would be shed. Maybe people would start getting some sleep now that the lights might not be flipped on and off at all hours of the night. Maybe we could start afresh with the tennis court. Maybe, just maybe, the 290 or so who were packed in here would be reduced to a reasonable number—or maybe (dream on) there might be a system put in place whereby inmates don't swelter in the summer and freeze in the winter.

But, as they say, be careful what you wish for.

Still, I couldn't keep from thinking that our prison—Montgomery Women's Facility—seems to be the dumping ground for what's leftover in the way of personnel and prisoners. After all, nobody is on death row in here—not that kind of place. This is literally a holding pen for people our antiquated legal system keeps churning out. Most are not bad enough to warrant extra security and yet not good enough to be let out into society, so they are in suspended animation, serving out their terms. The system doesn't have the time or the money to deal with them—and the prisoners keep coming and coming and coming.

That was my thought as I looked at Ms. Foley, but I said, "I think that's quite a compliment to you, Ms. Foley, that the warden wants your flowers."

"Don't I know it." And Ms. Foley was happily out the door.

Sara's special bookmarks, made exclusively for our book club!

CHAPTER 16

Now in Charge—
Three Lieutenants and a Captain

We are talking hot, hot, hot—ordinary for August.

As always, she was there waiting to help me unload. She marveled at my new car. I had traded after having the old one for twelve years. About time. When I tapped the knob to open the back hatch, she was so startled she had to jump back out of the way. Ms. Foley watched in awe as the rear door automatically lifted. "Ain't it amazin' what they're doin' with cars nowadays. I ain't never seen one like that—lift up all by itself."

I sometimes forget that if you've been out of circulation for years, you miss innovations that are now ordinary for the rest of us. I handed her a box of books. "Yeah, and ain't it amazing what they're charging for what they're doing with cars nowadays."

The guard, having inspected our haul, began walking slowly back to the gate. I handed Ms. Foley another bunch of books. She almost dropped them, as she was looking off toward the guard, to make sure he was out of earshot, I suppose. When she finally took the box, she turned to me and in a low voice, "I wanna tell you somethin'. I'm sorry to say it . . . but I'm thinkin' of tryin' to get a transfer up to that Birmingham Work Release place."

"What! What are you talking about, Ms. Foley? This place couldn't do without you."

"Can't get sleep enough to do my job. So much racket at night, can't close my eyes."

"You could get some ear plugs. I'll bring you . . ."

"And if I sleep too close to the wall, where all the smokers hang out, I smell like marijuana all the time. And in the summer, we burn up on the inside and the outside, and the guards are gettin' crazier and crazier, and in the winter when it rains, leakin' all over the place . . . Just getting to be too much." She dropped the extra books on our cart.

I was astounded—to even imagine this place without her. "What will they do without you around here? What about your flowers? What about your help in keeping the grounds?" And most of all, because it was purely a selfish thought, "What about our book club?"

She lifted another box of books on to our cart and smiled at my dismay. "I'm just sayin' I'm thinkin' 'bout it. Probably won't do nothin'—don't you worry none."

"Whew, you had me going there for a minute, Ms. Foley."

On our way in, I realized that the thing that must have precipitated her angst was this. Our warden of five months had now retired and was gone. Now there was a new system in place but not a new warden.

Now, each one of three lieutenants took a shift in charge. If anything serious happened—someone had to go to the hospital with health issues and an ambulance had to be called, or there was a serious fight, or whatever—then the captain had to be notified. Otherwise, the captain was not disturbed and the lieutenants were in charge. Where was the captain, you ask? One wonders. I assume, in and out.

Soon as we got into our meeting place, Val came up to me holding a scarf she had knitted for Sara. She was so proud of it, and she should have been. Knitting is one of the only relaxing pastimes here, and some of my book club members are very gifted knitters. It was lovely. I told her I knew Sara would be so surprised and pleased and I got Val's address. I knew Sara would want to write a thank-you note.

I was constantly touched by how much the book club gang seemed to connect with Sara and empathize with her. Attending when she could, she seemed to have developed a relationship with them that some had never had before. She never had anything but positive things to say about them—maybe akin to a mother figure they had never had.

On to the book this month. It's a true story, about a Jewish woman, who met a Nazi Party member during World War II. He fell in love with her, and despite her protests and her eventual confession that she was Jewish, he married her and kept her identity a secret. I just knew they would love this one. This was looking, up front, like it would be a good meeting, but just when I think I know what's going on . . .

As we ate, we began to talk about *The Nazi Officer's Wife*. Our twosome, Maya and Baby Cakes, said up front that they hadn't read our monthly read and then sat there, arms crossed, looking belligerent, expecting me to take exception, I suppose.

"Well, okay, then" was all I said, not wanting to cause a stir, never knowing what had happened in their lives between now and my last visit. I raised my eyebrows to Linda and passed on to others.

Harriettee, who was in for a short while before her van left for work at Fat Jack's Burgers, began by saying that she, for one, liked it, but "it was kinda hard to believe. She was a Jew and she married a Nazi and during World War II? Really? Was she crazy?"

Uma: "Yeah, she shoulda gone on and got out of there—and in a hurry. What in the hell was she thinkin'? Course now, I liked *In the Garden of Beasts* better." (Another recent read set in Germany, right before World War II.)

Maya and Baby Cakes still had not said anything, and every time somebody else said something, Baby Cakes and Maya cast a cynical eye in their direction.

And now that she had thought about it, Harriettee said she liked *Garden of Beasts* better too. Said the wife in *The Nazi Officer's Wife* just went along with the husband to survive—couldn't help it. "But that girl in *Garden of Beasts*—the ambassador's daughter—she was a real piece of work."

Evidently, by now, Maya and Baby Cakes had had enough. Their earlier pronouncement was meant to be a precursor to other thoughts and I hadn't picked up on it. Now Baby Cakes spoke up—arms still crossed. "All we ever be readin' in here is fightin' and warrin'. We want somethin' different—a funny one, or a romantic one."

"But I bring other books for y'all to read that I hope accommodate your particular interests . . . don't I?"

Baby Cakes sat there staring at the ceiling.

The others said nothing but began to be uneasy in their seats, eyes down. It then dawned on me that these two must have been appointed by the group to voice their objections.

I tapped my pencil on the table and went along. "Well, all-righty, then, I'll try to find something more . . . ," nodding to Baby Cakes and Maya, "more in line with your intellectual interests." And as an afterthought, "Uh, y'all realize that there are all sorts of interests in this group and I can't hit the spot every time."

They nodded and seemed mollified—for the moment. After all, I suppose you can't get too upset with the one who brings in the books and the food, else she might think twice about bringing in the books and the food next time. It occurred to me as I sat there and listened to the others talk about the book that I had never really heard them cuss or get vehement about anything much—other than prison conditions—when they came to book club. I suppose this was the most in the form of protest that I was ever likely to hear.

Later, when I got home, I looked up the books we had read centered around World War II and they were right: *Night, Unbroken, The Nazi Officer's Wife, Sarah's Key, In the Garden of Beasts.* Inadvertently I had picked, when I had a choice, what I thought was interesting and was not considering that they might not be as interested in history as me. In my defense, they had liked Sarah's Key and most had liked In the Garden of Beasts and, of course, Unbroken had been a smash hit. They had loved that. Now that I thought about it, I didn't feel so guilty, but the point was taken. Upon further consideration, I was happy that now they obviously cared enough about what they read in book club to be discerning.

Suddenly, right in the middle of our book discussion, the door to our meeting place opened and a guard walked in and everyone, except me, was asked to step out of the room. Seems there weren't enough guards on staff then so they were all doing double duty—checking things, and prisoners, that should have been checked earlier in the day, if there had been enough personnel to do it. I waited for about fifteen minutes and they all walked back in, having been checked, or vetted, or whatever. Seems this was part of the new system.

With three different lieutenants and a captain, the setup was ever chang-ing—depending on who was in charge at the moment. Upon checking in, I had asked if I might think about bringing in new tennis equipment and maybe relining the court now that there was a new administration of sorts. I wanted to think of Ms. Foley and the others out there playing again.

The lieutenant in charge, at the moment, had said an emphatic, "No." And that was the end of that.

Another change—a few months back we had been switched to another meeting room in the main administration building. This one is not con-ducive to walking out the door and smoking because it's inside and down a long hall, so it has cut down on the smoking, for the time we're in book club anyway. Maybe an inadvertent positive change.

It seems the place where we used to meet had been turned into the health center because the health center building was full of termites and had to be torn down.

Conditions were becoming more and more crowded. In addition to Ms. Foley's thinking of moving, for the first time, there was talk among the rest of my group of trying to get transfers up to the women's facility in Birmingham. It's also a work-release facility, but seems to have a bet-ter reputation than this one, not as overflowing as this one, and perhaps more well organized, and the rumor is that it has air-conditioning. Up until then, Birmingham Work Release was not a place you wanted to go. In fact, Uma had been there at one time, as had some of the others, and they had been happy to get to this place, but now the whole picture had changed . . .

A few days later, after our *Nazi Officer's Wife* reading, I received this letter from Linda. It seems that, among other things, Conner had gotten in some kind of big trouble where she worked in the governor's mansion and had been sent back to Tutwiler and put in seg—prison within the prison, where twenty-three of the twenty-four hours are spent in solitary confine-ment. You don't get sent to solitary for some small infraction. Must have been a major one.

With all the rush of news about Conner, there still seems to be more concern that our membership stays "even on color"—and who gets to take Conner's place.

Hay Pat,

I got your letter and I've passed it around to the others. We will be looking forward to seeing you on the 26th.

I've had two people ask me about joining our book club. They are both long timers like the rest of us. One is black and one is white. I told them that I would tell you about them so you could make a decision. We do have two spaces available and if both are chosen it would make it even on color.

Conner has been taken back to Tutwiler. She has gotten herself in some major trouble. They put her in a segregation cell under investigation. It would surprise me if they allow her to ever come back to this facility. I don't know the exact details but it was involving a black female officer that worked here.

And anyway, I've been getting a lot of flak from those who want in our book club about Conner not even coming to our meetings. I don't think the other members would mind the two who have asked me because they're good people but it's up to you. Their names are —— (white) and ——(black).

Let me know before book club or at book club. We can discuss it then if you choose.

Take care until we see you on the 26th.

Always, Linda

CHAPTER 17

Conner Busted

Upon entering, there was no gossip or talk of Conner's plight, or of new members who might be coming into the club—because a guard was present, filling up her water bottle with ice from the foam ice chest in the corner. We went straight to the book of the month.

They say that readers who like an old-fashioned saga will devour these sprawling novels of passion and revenge—that's according to *Library Journal*.

Okay, to salve my World War II guilt, a few months later I gathered together a bunch of the Leila Meacham novels. Some of her books had been in the boxes of used paperbacks that I had been bringing every month as extra reading. Pammie and Linda had said that they liked her stories, so . . .

I had gotten a chance to read one of them beforehand, and some interesting history was interwoven in there—ha.

Sara had come with me this time and basically, from the minute we came into our meeting room and began pulling together tables to have a conversation and eating area, we listened and listened and listened—so intent were they all on telling us the stories in the Meacham novels—or perhaps telling me how much they liked this kind of read as opposed to some of the others we had brought.

Sara and I would look at each other from time to time and shake our heads, smiling. They couldn't stop talking about the different stories they had read—and I think most all of them had read a number of the different Leila Meacham paperbacks I had brought in. Sara and I just sat there nodding our heads. They were so intent on the telling that we couldn't understand them half the time. Out came this heavy Black Belt accent from Uma and Baby Cakes especially, and so fast, and with colloquialisms that were so unfamiliar to us, that at times we couldn't follow. And who could interrupt to ask for an interpretation when the joy of the telling was so eager? Linda would look up parts and read short paragraphs. The others would nod at one thing they would all agree on or, in the next minute, get teary eyed at a plot point someone else would mention.

*

And wonder of wonders, after we had worn out the Meacham novels and were enjoying the last of the refreshments, Linda said to me that she had talked to the lieutenant in charge and, surprise, surprise, this lieutenant was now amenable to having tennis and getting our tennis court relined. She said she thought the inmates needed something to do and the exercise would be good for them. While she talked, I was remembering Pammie and her job of wiping down table number 3.

And, too, according to Linda, I had even gotten permission from this lieutenant to bring in more tennis equipment—extra balls and rackets. Good heavens!

So I would try to bring lining equipment next time I came, as most of the lines had faded away, and more tennis equipment . . . and hope the policy doesn't change by the time I show up again.

It must have been the nice fall weather—Harriettee, all smiles and still working at Fat Jack's Burgers, had gotten a parole date last month while I was gone. We had hoped it would happen. In for a short visit before she left for work, she said the manager of Fat Jack's Burgers said he would come and be a character witness at the parole hearing. She was thrilled and it seemed contagious. Our whole book club was happy for her and that is rare, because usually when someone gets a parole date, they keep it quiet. It is the opposite with Harriettee. I suppose they all felt she deserved it and that she had family support on the outside.

Sara and I sat there watching the other girls congratulate her and remembering when she first came. "Remember, Sara, when I had asked everyone to write down their daily schedule to get an idea of the life they lead in here? Some filled in time knitting or walking around the outdoor track, reading, or sleeping, or like Pammie, wiping down a table in the rec area—remember?"

"Yeah, I remember you told me Harriettee was working her fanny off in the kitchen."

"Well, she wasn't on it for too long, but it was the schedule that the newbies who qualify sometimes got assigned to."

And Sara, ever optimistic, said, "See, maybe there are some good things accomplished in here . . . by chance."

Here's Harriettee's daily schedule when she first came—as told by Harriettee:

2:00 a.m.—Waked up—by an officer that hates everything about his/her job—including the fact that he/she has to wake up, to wake me up.

2:00–3:00 a.m.—Drink two strong cups of black coffee—"violate" which is prison lingo for evade security long enough to smoke a cigarette because the smoke yard is not open until 7:00 a.m.

3:00–4:30 a.m.—Escorted to the kitchen to mix dough, cut dough and bake 600 biscuits by 4:30 a.m. to serve to the "population"

4:30–10:00 a.m.—Bake lunchtime bread (yeast rolls or cornbread) and make dessert for supper (cake, bread, sweet potato pie, cinnamon rolls, sugar cookies, etc.) and keep in mind, I must prepare enough for 300 inmates. On pancake day, each inmate gets three. I make 1,000 pancakes by 4:30 a.m. (this is only once a week—thank God)

10:00–11:00 a.m.—Back to the dorm, shower, and go to bed.

5:00–6:00 p.m.—Get up, drink two cups of coffee—(this is prerequisite to my becoming socially acceptable). Roll my cigarettes for the next day—go to mail call—answer mail if necessary—prepare to go to work the next day—get into bed by 8–9 p.m.—read until about 10 p.m. Back to sleep.

The euphoria of good news seems to always be tempered by the other news of the day, waiting in the wings—and now, finally, we heard the story of what happened to Conner.

Conner had gotten busted on the job at the governor's house. Conner, the one redeeming herself. Conner, our leader—no-nonsense Conner. Linda had written to me about it earlier but didn't give me any details. It was the first thing I had wanted to know after the chat-up about the Meacham novels and hearing Harriettee's good news. Finally, the guard had finished filling his water bottle, then stood around for a while, and then left.

"What happened?" I looked around to the others. "She was so thrilled with working there and she must have been doing a good job, knowing her penchant for organization."

"Conner, of all people." Even Sara, who had enjoyed their mutual interest in photography, was amazed.

Linda filled us in with what she had heard. It seems that Conner and one of the women guards were having an inappropriate relationship and got caught for that, along with being in possession of cell phones. The girls didn't seem to know all the particulars, only that she got sent back to Tutwiler and put in seg. You can't do much worse than to be sent to Tutwiler and then be put in seg to boot.

"And she was doing so well," I said, "and she was so happy." I couldn't understand why she would jeopardize her whole future. "What was she thinking?"

All eyes stared off in space or down at the table.

"It's like sliding back down a steep hill you've been climbing for years. Why do people go along making perfectly sane decisions, living in a tenuous situation anyway and knowing they are on the edge, and then do something dumb like that?"

"Maybe she was in love," a small voice from someone in the group.

I said, "What kind of love is it that trashes one of the lovers?"

Linda said, "One small consolation."

"I know, I know. You've said it before."

Linda: "Yeah, but it bears repeating."

"It doesn't help—not this time," I sighed.

Uma said, "It does if you the one incarcerated, Miss Pat, in-car-cer-a-ted. Makes *all* the difference."

Linda: "If the guard and the prisoner intertwine in any way, it is *always* the guard's fault."

Me: "Listen, y'all. Maybe sometimes it doesn't matter whose fault it was, if everybody gets screwed."

Baby Cakes—slapping her cheeks. "Did Miss Pat just say 'screwed'? I am shocked—shocked, I tell ya."

After we had all mulled it over a bit more, we ate and drank and the conversation wandered. Baby Cakes and Maya were talking again of leaving, if they could get a transfer up to Birmingham.

Rosalee had already gone up to Birmingham. I would imagine it was on the advice of her new husband. Can't blame him.

Now, even Keisha—our stellar member who went to trial instead of taking a plea bargain—was thinking of leaving, and she had always said she wouldn't be caught dead up in the Birmingham facility. She would wait for parole right here. Now, the picture had changed. "This place just sucks. You can't have one minute to yourself—unless you want to spend your life walking around the outdoor track. It's hot as hell in the summertime and the flies and bugs are on you all the time and to top it off, the guards . . ."

Linda sneered. "When did the guards ever know what they were doing?"

The talk meandered again. The governor's wife had come for a visit a few weeks back, and everything had to be spit-and-polish clean. All inmates had to sit on their respective bunks until she left. As a whole, they had liked her. Ms. Foley said she seemed like a nice person. Little did we know at the time, the governor's wife was on the verge of leaving the governor because of his philandering ways. Sometimes our public figures can be such sterling role models—yeah, right. Is it any wonder that this group in here might take issue with the purity of the law-abiding life they are told to emulate?

As Ms. Foley was passing out brownies for dessert, I decided to ask Keisha something I had wanted to ask for a long time but had not had the opportunity—this seemed like the moment. "So, Keisha, what type of murder are you in for? Was it auto related, as so many are?"

Keisha is not one to be bowled over by the system. Once before, when we were talking about plea-bargaining and most everyone else said they had taken a plea bargain and regretted it, Keisha looked at us with unblinking presence and said, "I have told y'all before, I would never take a plea bargain. I insisted on going to trial."

Now, she smiled, condescendingly. "To answer your question, Pat. What got me in here was, partying—too hard." And she smiled again as she lifted her glass and nonchalantly tipped it to me.

And I said, just as off-hand, "Well, that hard partying can do it," which immediately solicited guffaws from all the others.

Linda scoffed. "Yeah, right, Pat, like you know one single thing about partying."

I nodded and smiled, taking a drink of lukewarm water, once again marveling at the distance between us. "You're absolutely right. I don't know one single thing about partying—partying hard . . . if it's liable to end up getting you killed."

Then, of course, the whole group erupted with laughter, trying to imagine Pat, the nerd, partying hard.

Later, as Sara and I were driving home up I-85 in the afternoon traffic, I couldn't get Conner, and her trouble at the governor's house, off my mind. And unexpectedly, I was now disgusted with her.

"How could she do that? She was being such an example to us all. Even the good warden we had long ago, the one who had sent her there, trusting she would justify his confidence. What in the hell was she thinking?" I turned off 85 and headed north toward the rolling hills of central Alabama.

Sara was watching the afternoon sun settle into the Alabama pines. "Did you notice how Linda kept tapping her pencil on the table and sighing in commiseration, perhaps too loudly, every time somebody said something about Conner?"

"I hadn't thought of that. Do you think so?"

Sara nodded. "As I watched Linda and the others in there today, I realized there might be a part of them that was thinking, 'Hey, she got her chance and she screwed it up, whereas I would have done better than that. I would have done the right thing. Now she'll never get out of here— serves her right.'"

"You're right. I guess I couldn't blame them, if they did think that." I turned right onto a backroad that is a shortcut bypassing the town of Tallassee and weaving down into the woods and around the remains of an old Confederate rifle factory. "I still can't understand Conner's thinking . . . or upon reflection, maybe I can." I stopped to let a deer have his way crossing the road—better than having his way with my car.

Sara said, "If you've never really been loved—even as a child you never felt love—that reassuring confidence that comes from knowing you are important in someone else's eyes, then maybe that's your life's unending quest, whether you realize it or not."

I let a raccoon meander across behind the deer before starting up again. Sara is an avowed environmentalist and so when she is in the car, I always bow to nature.

Sara let down her window to shoo the raccoon on its way. "And if you finally find someone that you think loves you, then to hell with getting out of jail and living your life. This is the here and now, and I have to grab it or it may not come ever again."

"If that's what happened."

"Yeah, if that's what happened."

We came up out of a tangle of kudzu to turn right and cross the bridge that spans the Tallapoosa River. To our left, the huge dam that holds back millions of gallons. Only two of its spillways were open, letting the water out in thin measured streams.

CHAPTER 18

Linda Schools the Guards

Cold and damp as we pass by on the way into the visitor's room.

This month's read is set in France and is about a charismatic con man who befriends a disabled French aristocrat and becomes his caregiver—*You Changed My Life*. Evidently a movie has been made about his life that was a blockbuster in Europe. A good story, but more to our point, there are parts about his life in the French prison system that I thought would be interesting and enlightening to my gang—not to mention that I got copies in paperback at the Dollar Tree—for a dollar each. Yes! My kinda read.

In one particular chapter the main character has been sentenced to serve time in one of the more progressive jails in France and he describes what prison life was like—perhaps sardonically, but close to the truth.

And my gang was not buying it.

Linda: "I don't believe it. He had a room all to himself when he went to prison? And it wasn't seg? Are you kidding me?"

Me: "Well, in France and in some other European countries . . ."

Val: "And a TV all his own? Give me a break! And coulda watched it anytime he wanted to? Really. I am not believing one word of this story."

Me: "Well, you see, over there, the prison system is . . ."

Uma: "And he gets coffee *delivered* to him in the mornin'? Did you read that part, in chapter 15, I think? Not for one minute is that true. *We* the ones live in the greatest country in the world. Not true, not true."

Linda: "And did you read where the guard *asks* him if he wants to go outside and exercise? Oh, please." She gets up to demonstrate, playing the guard. "Excuse me, ladies, but would y'all like to come on out and walk around the track today or perhaps play a little tennis?"

Gales of laughter—and Baby Cakes: "I just can see Lieutenant Jenson askin' us if we wanna take a walk."

Pammie: "Yeah—just think about it. If old Jenson ever asked us if we wanna to take a walk, it wouldn't be outside to the track. We liable never to be seen again."

Baby Cakes: "Sounds like livin' in luxury, like in a Holiday Inn. I should be so lucky."

Harriettee—in for a short visit before heading to the work van—but still having read the book of the month: "And the meals—I'll bet he had crepe suzettes every day for breakfast, made by the prison chef—oh, sure."

Pammie: "Crepe who?"

Harriettee: "Kinda like pancakes, darlin'."

Pammie: "How about Big Macs? Think they got those in France?"

Ms. Foley: "I like the part where he come to be friends with the man in the wheelchair. Done had some fun adventures with him—and him bein' paralyzed from the neck down." She smiled at the others, who stared back at her, amazed that she seemed to have missed the entire point of the whole story. Or perhaps she had gotten the entire point, but I didn't comment—just listened, having given up trying to explain away parts of the prison system in France.

Uma: "Right, Ms. Foley, that was a nice part of the story." Uma sighed and looked off to a distant horizon silhouetted by the Eiffel Tower. "Good food, morning coffee, and a room to yourself. Goin' to France soon as I get outta here."

I suppose that what is the truth, as seen through the lens of your everyday ongoing experience, can easily not be the truth.

I had thought that with the coming dawn of a new year maybe everyone would be more upbeat, waiting for the momentary arrival of yet another new warden, checking off another year served, but that was not the case. After we finished our discussion of the book of the month, it was back to our jaded jail. Now everyone was complaining about the facility—the guards were jerks—the food was awful—even the canteen lady had been fired—rumor had it that she had an inappropriate relationship with one of the inmates. At least that was the supposed reason for firing her. Ms. Foley said that was not so. "One of the guards had it in for the canteen lady and got her fired."

Everyone, well, almost everyone, who can qualify now wants to be sent to the Birmingham Work Release facility. Baby Cakes and Maya have finally finagled transfers up to Birmingham and will be leaving soon—and I will miss their presence at book club.

Still no new warden.

In an attempt to lighten the mood, I pulled a small plastic bag out of my satchel and handed it to Linda. "Ta-daaa." She had written me that she had broken her glasses frames and might not be able to finish the book, but of course she had anyway—and I had taken the hint and brought in three pairs of reading glasses from a Dollar Tree for her to choose from. She was delighted and said she would have one of them altered to fit her prescription lenses.

"I don't think that's such a good idea, Linda. If you try it yourself, you'll crack the lens, at the very least. Then you won't have anything left—prescription or reading."

Ms. Foley took off her glasses and passed them down the table to me. "My frames done broke back in July and looka here." I took a look and tried them on. They were prescription and fitted to dollar store frames—precisely fitted to dollar store frames.

"Bobbie Jean, she done it for me," Ms. Foley said. "She's been in here goin' on what—ten year now? Fixes everybody's glasses."

And sure enough, whoever Bobbie Jean is, she knows her stuff. All sorts of occupations in Montgomery Women's Facility. I didn't bother to ask where she got the files to do her work. That would only require answers and invest me with knowledge that I don't want to have.

Big news of the day—Val had been assigned to take Conner's place at the governor's mansion. For some time now, Val had been counting on EOS, and the date was coming closer and closer with each tick of the clock. It'd been fifteen years since the vehicular homicide that landed her in here. She wouldn't get out for a few more months, and in that time, she would be working at the governor's house. I suppose the theory was that since she already had her ticket out, she wouldn't dare mess it up by committing any infractions. I was, of course, happy for her, but I would miss her, as she knew all the ins and outs of this place, and from now on, she wouldn't be here if I had questions. Also, I'd miss her neatly typed sheets of inventoried books I've brought in.

As I was congratulating Val on her new job and trying on various other glasses passed to me by other members of the group that had been expertly filed down to fit their dollar store glasses sent from home, Betty wandered in, cane in hand, looking rather pale but smiling.

"Well, look what the cat drug in." Linda pulled up a chair for Betty to hobble to, and after a shaky sit-down, Betty told her story. Seems that while she was at Tutwiler, supposedly getting drug free again, she had tried to step off her top bunkbed and had broken her leg in the fall.

She told me—the others already having heard—that for a while she had been in a wheelchair, but since then she had graduated to a walker, and now "this here cane." She leaned it against her leg and stared at it. "Come a long way from my mama bringin' me meals in my home jail."

How, I wondered, can one be drug free and step off a top bunk and break her leg to such an extent that she had to use a wheelchair? But since we were right in the middle of talking about glasses, I didn't have a chance to really speak with her and find out more. I wish now I had taken the time when she was with us.

Later, as I was leaving, Linda told me that Betty hadn't mentioned it, but that while she was in Tutwiler, she had received news that her youngest son had died—killed himself or a drug overdose, she wasn't sure which.

I grimaced, remembering how many times Betty had told me about her sons, how much she loved them, and that it was her one big regret—not being able to be with them.

On to happier notes—tennis. Since I had been given permission by this particular captain, I had, once again, borrowed tennis lining equipment and had, once again, brought it with me, along with balls and a new racket or two, courtesy of the U.S. Tennis Association. When it was time to go out to the court to fix the lines and see how their tennis was coming along, I showed a printed copy of the email from the captain, trying to abide strictly by the rules—whatever they might be for this particular day. The front office took a distant look and waved me out with a guard escort. When we got down to the court with the girls, the guard said she was leaving to get something to eat. She hadn't had any lunch.

Fine with me. I nodded and she left.

A little while later, as we were finishing up the lining, a new guard showed up, perturbed to the point of apoplexy. "What in the world are you doing out here—and without a guard? You're supposed to have a guard escort with you at all times."

"Well, the guard that brought me out here said she had to go to lunch and she left. I guess she'll be back in a while." I turned to watch the lining process. Linda had popped a line and Pammie was trying to follow it with the football lining gizmo.

My explanation hadn't seemed to placate the guard—going for his pencil like he was drawing a sword. "What's your name?" I told him and he began to write. "Get up. I have to take you out right now. You can't be out here without a guard."

"But you're out here and you're a . . ."

That only made him madder.

I tried to explain again. "Sir, the captain gave me permission to do this. Can't you wait until we're finished with the lining equipment? I have to take it back with me as I go. I borrowed it."

"No, you can't wait. Get your stuff and get up. I need to get you out of here right now."

At this point Linda and Pammie ambled over to save me. Linda said quietly to the guard, "You see that truck over there, sir, the one outside the exercise yard fence?"

The guard pretended to keep writing but did glance up—and then back to his official papers, scribbling away.

"That truck has a guard in it, maybe even two guards. It is out there to watch everything that goes on in the exercise yard. He'll take care of things. Don't you worry." Linda had on her best mother hen voice.

The guard grumbled a few more comments, then turned and left.

Linda patted me on the shoulder. "He's a newbie. He'll learn his way around."

Pammie: "Takes 'em a while and by that time, they either get transferred to another facility or quit. Then we start all over again." She immediately corrected herself: "*Linda* teaches 'em how to behave. I don't get caught up in that sort of thing. Ain't none of me."

"Well, thank goodness y'all are here. If you hadn't been, he might be dragging me out by my hair."

I turned back to watch the girls who were now warming up for a game on our newly lined court. All the while I was thinking that it was getting to be like the old novel, *One Flew over the Cuckoo's Nest.* First you are given permission to have tennis—then no, you can't have tennis—then yes, sure, you can have tennis. It'll be good for the inmates—but do it like we tell you—which all depends on who tells you—and at what time.

We were all hoping the new warden would get things organized enough that the left hand would know what the right hand was doing.

Later, when it was time for me to go, the guard came out, chatting and friendly this time, to escort me to the gate. He had me follow him straight through the sleeping area jammed with bunkbeds. I had been told that it was against the rules for outsiders to go through the bunk area, instead of around the outside of the building, but I didn't have the heart to tell him.

We did have a fun time out there in the yard, watched over by the invisible faces in the truck outside the fence. Our little mini round robin seemed to be enjoyed by everybody. Even the group of sixty or seventy women who were sitting on the grass knoll overlooking our court, smoking and intermittently watching, seemed to enjoy it. Ms. Foley even consented to having a partner some of the time. And of course, she had her knee pads on—running back and forth over her little court kingdom, the others taking turns trying to outlast her—to no avail.

The prisoners playing by their own rules

Some of the girls lining the tennis courts to their personal specifications

CHAPTER 19

The Redneck Mafia

A new warden! I can't believe it. We had a new warden, not just captains and lieutenants but a real-life warden and a new day—and another truism: Be careful what you wish for.

She wasn't out on the grounds as I drove up. Then I spotted Ms. Foley off at a safe distance, sitting on the steps of the healthcare building, holding on to her cart, waiting. Seems the new warden dictated that she couldn't help me unload because she couldn't come outside the fencing anymore. Forget that for ages she had spent hours outside the perimeter fencing, cutting grass with heavy machinery, loading and unloading books, and other work. I guess now she was too dangerous. On second thought, I shouldn't have been so judgmental. After all, it was a new day—maybe.

I went to the guard house to hand in my license and check in. The guard told me that I must unload by myself from now on, which is fine with me—no problem. "Good," she said, "but first empty out your pockets and take off all your jewelry and take off that sweater you have on and leave your watch in your car." Then we went back to the old body search for visitors. I was taken into the bathroom and searched.

Okay, I said to myself. Isn't that usual for a prison? It is, but it had not been in here. On long ago visits to Tutwiler, I was required to do all of this in addition to shaking out my bra to make sure I wasn't carrying contraband, but Tutwiler is Tutwiler. This place had been a different story, a work-release facility, up until now. And maybe this new method, this added security, would be better. I don't know. Now the assistant warden was called in, and I was told to go get the book of the month and bring it to her.

"Just the book of the month? None of the others I bring in for extras?"

"No, none of the others. Just the book of the month."

"All-righty, then."

I went and got a copy out of my car and brought it to her. She looked it over very thoroughly, leafing through the pages, and eventually seemed to be satisfied and handed it back to me.

"Okay," she said, and she left. The other guards in the check-in room shrugged and went back to work. I guess she was satisfied that I wasn't having my group read inappropriate material or stashing any drugs or bringing in pornographic subjects—or whatever. Forget the other nine copies I've brought—and all the extras.

By this time, when I went back outside, Ms. Foley had inched up to the fencing with her cart, which she sheepishly pushed to me through the gate.

"Sorry."

"No problem, Ms. Foley. Not any of your doin', girl."

I unloaded the books, the eight salads I brought from Burger Joe's and the eight fruit yogurt parfaits, along with the homemade brownies. Also, a box of used paperbacks and a stack of used magazines. Then I dragged the cart in through the gate, with Ms. Foley and other members of the book club watching but not allowed to help. This could portend good things—new regulations, consistent with competent new leadership.

Once inside the visitation center room—first things first. My come-to-Jesus meeting, before we got to the book of the month.

For some time now, I had noticed a more and more lackadaisical attitude, as if they individually had no responsibility. They might read the book of the month or they might not—depending on the mood they were in. After all, it was only old Pat bringing in the books, and what trouble could that be? Besides, refreshments were the main thing. Of course, there was always the core group that read the book, and several others besides. But there were others, like Val, working in the office all the time and now at the governor's house—and Pammie. I've not a clue what she did all day, besides wipe down table number 3. They might or might not have read the book of the month.

In my lecture, I didn't name names, but I did give my sermon about being responsible—about how more people than just me were involved in this venture. My sisters—one making brownies each time and transcribing their writings, the other gathering books from up in the North Georgia mountains where she lives and trekking them back down south—the various libraries that hold books back for us. Friends and neighbors who saved old magazines so they could be entertained.

And when I was finished, Linda, of course, spoke for the whole group. The others sat there—heads bowed. Linda dutifully said that I was right and that they would do better and that they didn't realize so many other people were involved.

Probably didn't do a damn bit of good but it made me feel better. In here as on the outside, there are some who will toe the line and others who want to slide by. Just a different degree of toeing and sliding in here . . . I suppose.

I looked around for Betty and then asked—"Tutwiler?"

"No, Birmingham."

"Birmingham? Did she ask to go up there?"

"No, she was sent."

"Maybe that's for the best."

When I had the time to go to the Web and look up stipulations for sending stuff to her new prison, I'd mail Betty the last answers to her questions that my sister typed up for her autobiography. It was the one thing she seemed genuinely interested in.

I know I didn't see them on a daily basis, but after seven years it was strange that some of the regulars were gone now and I probably wouldn't ever see them again or know how they are faring.

So, of my original gang, who did we have left here? Since I was here last, Harriettee had finally gotten out on parole, and well deserved—I hope she won't be back. Betty was now drugging it up in B'ham. Baby Cakes and Maya had gotten their transfer up to Birmingham as well. And Conner was still at Tutwiler, they said.

Now we were down to five of our original founding members:

Linda—the librarian turned recording secretary. She had become the voice of our book group, taking time to write me with the news of the day and the opinions of the day. I could always count on her.

Ms. Foley—still tending to her gardens.

Uma—our budding entrepreneur, running her own businesses inside these walls (I don't ask) and always ready with a funny story. The word is that she needed the money to help with college expenses for her daughter. Whether true or not, it does sound lovely.

Pammie—who goes along to get along, forever wiping down table number 3.

And Keisha—no-nonsense Keisha, who wouldn't take a plea bargain—no matter what awaited her.

Val was still in the system but didn't take part in book club anymore as she was at the governor's house working most of the time.

So we had decided in our last meeting to invite one new visitor each month. We weren't asking them to join, just come and tell us their story and read the book of the month along with us and enjoy the refreshments.

And my new tactic—we would have the book discussion *before* we ate this time—and sure enough, I did get more discussion.

First, Uma gave a long and interesting report on her book—one that she had asked me to look for and that I had recently found in paperback and given to her last month—*Incidents in the Life of a Slave Girl*, a narration by an enslaved woman back in the day. Uma gave a wonderful accounting of the book everyone seemed to enjoy. We clapped when she finished.

It seems that with the coming of the new warden, Uma had lost her primary job, maybe her only job, as the official photographer. The camera was now too expensive to be entrusted to an inmate, although in times past it had been assigned to various other inmates. (Remember when Conner took wedding pictures?) This didn't seem to faze Uma. "Gives me more time to do my thing, and hey, y'all remember Pammie's job. Just as soon not have one as that one."

My mind momentarily wandered as I remembered a conversation I'd had about Uma with two of my book club women as they were walking me back to the exit gate after one recent meeting. No guard escort this time, and so the talk was free flowing.

"I hear," I said, "that Uma is one of the uh . . . masterminds in here. I know there must be lots of them, and yet I never see any sign of her using."

Ms. Foley explained. "Course not, Ms. Pat, she don't use. Just get it for everybody else and make a good amount doin' it—so they say." Ms. Foley immediately began to backtrack, not wanting to put the direct finger on anyone. "Course if she was a person like that—selling drugs, don't ya know—if she was somebody like that, it mighta helped out to keep up her children, don't ya know." Ms. Foley looked to the other two, who commiserated by nodding their heads, seeming sympathetic to Uma's attempts—no matter how misplaced—to help her family. And the others said, almost in unison, "*If* she did that sorta thing, which we ain't sayin' she does . . . did . . . will do."

I have to keep telling myself that in here, we live by an entirely different code of ethics. You may have been convicted of murder or manslaughter, but you are redeemed if you try to put your mischiefs to good use—no matter the method of doing it. And of course, there is the ever-present fear of retribution, if you go snitching on one of the power brokers.

And I said, "So how does that work—I mean—if she was one of the ones doing it? If she was, she just can't sell some drugs in here and then get the money and send it home to her family . . . can she?" I tried for my most innocent expression, knowing that they take great pleasure in educating me.

Ms. Foley: "Well, now, the way it is, Miss Pat—the way it *might be*, is this: She has her customers in here pay her back in MoneyGrams from they friends on the outside, and then they send that money on to her family, which is on the outside, don't ya know . . . if she, or anybody else, was to do it, which I ain't sayin' she does—or they might."

I sighed—"The good old American entrepreneurial spirit."

Ms. Foley: "The what?"

Me: "Well, it would be like Bernie Marcus not wanting to sell Home Depot stuff to a convention of home builders. Uma has a captured market in here, so to speak."

Ms. Foley: "Bernie who?"

"You know—he started Home Depot."

Ms. Foley: "Ain't heard tell of him. Can't say as I heard of the Home Depot neither."

As Pammie squirmed in the seat beside me, my mind was jerked back to the present ongoing conversation—Pammie's day job in here.

Pammie was grinning. "What's you talkin' 'bout, Uma? It ain't easy wiping down table number 3 every day—sometimes twice a day . . . or three times—but somebody gotta do it."

Ms. Foley: "Some don't have no jobs, Miss Pat."

Linda: "I have a better job than Pammie—really, it is better. I love it because it gives me some time to be by myself, and in here that's pure luxury." Somehow, Linda wasn't the librarian anymore. I don't know how that came about, but it is as it is. Later I asked and was told there was no librarian anymore.

Me: "So what is it—this new job of yours?"

Linda: "Cleaning out the phone booths. You know, the phone booths outside of the dorm, where people can make calls to loved ones."

Keisha: "Or to the parole board office." Keisha high-fives Uma.

Linda: "Shut up, Keisha. She didn't mean a thing by that, Pat. Pay her no mind."

I looked around at the others. They were looking at the ceiling or down at their fingers. I knew by then, this means stop—and I did. I saved that inquiry for another day. "All-righty, then. On to our guest of the month."

Our visiting guest was introduced—Dora Van. Seems Dora had been in several years and knew the ropes, so I was told, and she was more than happy to tell her story.

It was this: She was framed, that's why she was in here. The Redneck Mafia did it.

I looked around at the grinning others.

Me—trying to go along. "Gee, can't say I've heard of the Redneck Mafia." I try to say it in a polite way, so as not to incite unease. "I've heard of the Dixie Mafia, but not the Redneck Mafia . . . so far."

Keisha, amused but not surprised: "You said yourself, Pat, you're green about stuff in here."

I readily admitted it, with a nod and a shrug. Meanwhile, our guest proceeded to tell us, in all earnestness, that the Redneck Mafia was everywhere and that at this moment, they were trying to get to her in here, in prison, and shut her up, even though she was not guilty of what they said she was guilty of—which was killing her husband. We were then subjected to a half hour of information about her case. She had tried in vain to extricate herself from the Redneck Mafia's clutches, but all the while the Redneck Mafia was on her trail—even in here. Our guest went on and on about the various tricks the Redneck Mafia was using to trap her into confessing.

Meanwhile, I was beginning to rethink our new guest of the month policy.

After another thirty minutes, our guest had run out of things to tell us and so, having made her case, she was free to have the refreshments. Later, when I asked who suggested this guest, Uma raised her hand. "Knew you would get a kick out of her. Wish Miss Sara'd been here too, for this one. She'd a loved this one."

"She was interesting. I'll give you that—perhaps a little in the burned brain category, but very nice." I nodded to Uma and smiled. And I was thinking to myself, *burned brain*—even I am using the correct vernacular now.

Lately, Sara had not been up to coming on a regular basis, but she liked to keep in touch, and the book club loved hearing from her.

Quite a few of the gang had asked about her each time I came without her, and after many inquiries, I felt an explanation was in order and only fair to them, so I began the inevitable talk.

"It's like this, y'all. In her condition you all know that she has two choices. Keep trying new medications as long as they are available or stop her medication, and that usually has a hard outcome. She's been dealing with it for eight years now. I know it was a hard decision for all of us, but it was hers to make."

The news was greeted with silence, and I had thought at the time that there had been minimal recognition of what that meant, but then this note from Linda—our book club spokesperson—arrived in Sara's mail a few days after my last visit.

Dear Sara,

The battle you have chosen now will have a high price, but so are the rewards, and then there's victory. Please know that I regard you with the upmost respect.

I hope that you don't mind that Pat shared with our group about your decision to end the torment of the chemicals to your body.

Forgive me if I don't know exactly what to say, but all I know is that I had to say something. Because you matter to me.
Thank you for giving me the pleasure of knowing such a wonderfully strong woman. You have brought me light into the dark world I have to live in right now.

I shall cherish you always. May peace be with you.

Linda

When I think back about it, I wonder sometimes if Sara's example of how to conduct a life was more important than all the books, trinkets, and other paraphernalia I had been dragging in to them over the years.

She truly did exemplify a life well lived and under circumstances that helped put their prison lives in perspective.

CHAPTER 20
Lessons Learned on *The Road*

Finally, along with our guest speaker, we ate our refreshments (the salads were getting warm) and discussed my main reason for being here—our book of the month—Cormac McCarthy's classic:

The world as we knew it is gone, and a few stragglers of humanity are left to wander *The Road*.

Most seemed to have read all of it or some of it. So, during the discussion period, I posed the obvious question to them. "What would you have done if there was nothing left of the world you had known?"

Keisha—the hardheaded one who had insisted on going to trial—was first up. "Well, Pat, if the civilized world came to an end, like it did in the book, I'd just as soon die along with everybody else—not slog along the road, like the man and his boy did." The others nodded in emphatic agreement.

I did not mention that years in a prison, slogging along, with no end in sight, with no goals to be accomplished or even considered, might have some parallel.

I asked them about a theme of the novel: "What does 'we carry the fire' mean?" It was a line that the main character used throughout the story, to suggest that he and the little boy were the last purveyors of civilization as they knew it. All seemed to have an idea of the theme but didn't seem to feel any responsibility for saving civilization, until we turned the theme homeward, into their world.

Me: "Do y'all carry the fire in here? In here in the prison, some of you have jobs to keep the place running, don't you? And what would happen if you didn't do your jobs?"

They sighed and gave me dubious looks, but I could tell they were beginning to think about it.

Me: "Why, heck, y'all even tell the guards what to do when they're new and don't know the ropes. Remember, Linda, that time we were out in the exercise yard doing tennis and you had to explain to the new guard how things worked or he very well could have thrown me out?"

Linda, nodding slowly: "Yeah, you're right, I do that. I sometimes have to explain to the new ones what's going on . . . until they get to know the place and then they start acting like asses."

Pammie: "And then that one leaves and a new one comes in and we start the training all over again."

Me: "Remember what Harriettee told us she did when she first came in here? She and her kitchen people cooked a lot of the food?"

Pammie, staring off into the past, remembering her first days of incarceration: "Yeah, I used to work in the kitchen too, when I first come. Did all that stuff—'fore I started wipin' a table."

Me: "Y'all clean up your own living area and clean up the administration office and the bathrooms and the phone booths and wipe down the tables. And remember the time you told me about, Pammie? When you had to keep one of the short-timers from using the same rag to wipe down the microwave as she was using to clean out the toilets? Yuck. Remember?"

Pammie: "I had to. Nobody else was doin' it. Guards didn't give a shit—wasn't their microwave."

Ms. Foley: "And the grounds, we keep the grounds lookin' nice and pretty."

Uma: "They so shorthanded in here, if we didn't watch out for everybody, wouldn't be no *here* to begin with."

There was a silence as they considered. After a moment, they all began to chime in.

Uma: "Why, yeah, we do. We carry the fire, Miss Pat, we sure do. Keep this place goin' and we do all the work and the others [the short-timers], they don't do nothin'."

Pammie: "I just wipe down the table, but it's a table that don't get wiped if I don't do it." She leaned back in her chair. "Yeah, we do carry the fire. In here, we do. All them short-timers and some of them guards, just people along the road."

※

News of the day—of the fading day:

Even Ms. Foley—even Ms. Foley—says she has been accepted to go to Birmingham. "This place is so noisy—can't sleep. And if ya can't sleep, ya can't get nothin' done and the guards gettin' meaner every day and the plumbing don't work half the time."

It seems, so they told me, that the dorm was divided into sections: work-release people, people not on work release, back wall people (reserved for marijuana smokers), and factory people (who work at Tutwiler during the day). With it all, there was just too much chaos, even for Ms. Foley, even to the point that she was willing to leave her beautiful garden grounds.

Linda had tried to dissuade her. "Ms. Foley, why don't you wait a few months and let things cool off. Maybe the new warden will get things going better—or maybe she'll retire. We can always hope."

I sat there listening to the chatter and thinkng that if Ms. Foley went, I might think about calling it quits myself. She was one of my originals. I'd come to think of her as a friend. I'd served my time too and wouldn't feel any guilt about leaving them to fend for themselves—book-wise, that is. Right, Pat, not much, you wouldn't. Then again, I keep hoping that things will get better in the way we serve this population.

With everyone leaving or trying to, I realized for the first time that it had been over a year since Linda had asked me for a letter of commendation, back when she was trying for parole. After I gave it to her, extolling her skills as the librarian, I never heard anything else about it. And she never mentioned it again. Obviously, she must have gotten turned down.

As long as I was taking a mental count, I asked about Conner. Had anyone heard what had become of her since she got busted at the governor's mansion and sent back to Tutwiler?

Someone in the group said that they thought Conner would be coming back here, one of these days.

Me: "Conner, back here? I thought they had put her under the jail at Tutwiler."

"Remember the rule, Pat. Anytime a guard and . . ."

Me: "Yeah, yeah, I know."

Linda: "They say she's out of seg now."

I told the group I wouldn't be here the next month because I was going to have a hip replacement—too many years of tennis and jogging—and they said that old Miss Nellie, who had been here in prison for years, had just had a hip replacement, and that when she came back to the prison, she got busted for having heavy drugs in her system.

As I packed to leave, we all had a big chuckle over poor Miss Nellie, laughing over her absurdly ridiculous predicament.

Me: "After that operation, I'm so glad she *did* have drugs in her system."

Linda: "Wonder if she got as much tacked on to her sentence as I did when I . . . messed up."

Ms. Foley: "No—for real, after a while they done realized what they done to Miss Nellie and righted it."

I hadn't thought about Linda's history for some time, until she mentioned having "messed up." My curiosity bubbled up again. For the most part I know about my individual members' past only through their eyes. All Linda had ever told me was that she had escaped one time. That night after the meeting, I punched up my laptop and looked back through the archives of the *Montgomery Advertiser*, Montgomery's largest newspaper, and there it was—a news report about what happened. Seems that she and another prisoner walked off the work-release site they were on and stole a car—after her partner in crime stabbed the owner of the car to death. They ended up being caught in Texas, when they didn't have enough money to buy gas and tried to steal it.

How unsettling it is to suddenly become aware of someone's dreadful past after knowing them in an entirely different light for so long. Okay, I knew she was in prison for crimes committed, but I knew her as Linda the Librarian, the one who organized everything, who corresponded with me about meeting times, who sent caring notes to Sara, who seemed to be so supportive of her fellow inmates. And now, the one person who would probably never get out of here. In light of that newspaper story I read, I wouldn't give her one chance in a million.

No wonder she hadn't asked me for another recommendation letter. I suppose it would probably have been worthless.

Would we all be flabbergasted if we could suddenly tear open our friends, or family members' pasts and discover things we hadn't known?

CHAPTER 21

Our Treacherous Brownies
Are Banned

May is a nice time of year down here. The weather is warm but hasn't turned blazingly hot yet. It must have been the guard I got this time, not much hassle. She just glanced at the extra books I had brought—plus the salads, yogurt, the brownies—and after a few pleasantries waved me through. Things must be settling down.

Uma was standing just inside the fencing to help me with the cart. Uma? Why not Ms. Foley? I do know that Uma seems to have powers the others don't have. Don't ask me why the rules were suddenly and temporarily changed. I haven't a clue. And no, there was not a guard with us as escort. The guard who checked me in watched from the gate but didn't escort us. Shorthanded, or are they beginning to get reorganized around here?

But wait. I should not have concerned myself with this temporary civility. It was quickly erased. As we walked across the grounds, another guard rushed up to me—glaring, hands on hips—and began berating me for having taken a picture outside the gate. As I had been driving up to the facility this time, I had slowed down to take a picture of the five or six metal buildings surrounded by barbed wire that make up the MWF. I was trying to get a picture of Ms. Foley's flowers that dot the grounds, to show to a volunteer who donates her old gardening magazines. I was still in my car and had not yet passed through the gate into the parking area, but this guard must have seen me and taken exception—or had nothing better to do.

"But I thought it would be all right since I was still on the outside road . . ."

"No. You ain't got a right to take pictures—*any time.*"

"Yes, but I wasn't even out of my car and the window was rolled up . . . and it's a public road—isn't it?"

Never mind that in times past, I had been given permission by the old warden to take pictures inside the gate, on special occasions. This guard was determined to show me, and all those watching, that he was The Man.

And the amazing thing to me was that I was not the least bit fazed anymore by this kind of treatment. I felt like saying—but did not—"Yeah, yeah, so get on with it, kid. I have work to do." Instead, I stood there until he had finished—told him I certainly wouldn't do it again—and then walked on.

As Uma and I headed toward our meeting room, I was reminded of our last gathering when someone—Linda, I believe—had said to shut up about the parole board office, and knowing that Uma knows all, I asked.

But first a little flattery. "So, Uma, being as how you are the wise, all-knowing head honcho of this place, will you tell me something?"

"You name it, Miss Pat."

"Why did Keisha give you a high-five when she mentioned the parole office last time we were having a meeting and then suddenly Linda was so adamant about getting y'all to stop talking about it?"

Uma grinned. "Old Keisha—gone on up to Birmingham—and she say she would never go."

Me: "Keisha too—damn. Wait a minute, you're changing the subject, Uma. What is it with you and the parole board office?"

Uma patted me on the back. "You gotta know the ropes, Miss Pat."

"If anybody knows the ropes, you do."

Uma nodded. "True. Well, here's the way I work it. See, I wanna get out of here soon as I can and so I keep callin' the parole board office to see what I can find out—you know, like when my parole hearing might be coming up, things like that."

"That sounds logical. What do they say?"

Uma looked to the sky and shook her head. "Fact of the matter is, Miss Pat, inmates can't just up and call the parole board office. They'd be half the inmates in the prisons all over Alabama callin' 'em up."

"Good point."

"So, here's how I do it. I call my sister, and then she keeps me on the line and she calls the parole board office and when they comes on the line, I do the talkin', pretendin' I'm my sister, only I got to do it in a hurry cause every fifteen minutes, the prison switchboard comes on the line and says, 'This call is comin' from the prison,' or somethin' like that." Uma couldn't help but laugh at her creativity. "So, the trick be to keep it short."

"Even though it's illegal in the first place?" I asked.

"Gotta fend for yourself in here. But you gotta be careful."

"And if you get caught?"

"But I don't get . . ."

We had come to the door of the administration building. Our conversation abruptly ended as we pushed our goodies past the guard office and down the hall to our meeting room.

Ms. Foley and the rest of our members had to wait at a distance until we got everything in and then were able to come help with setup in the visitation room.

This time in, as we were unpacking, I was greeted with the news that more and more of our original book club members were leaving. I know it was selfish of me to even think of begrudging them their chance to have something better, even if it was just up to the Birmingham Work Release facility or better yet, EOS, but it'd been seven years since we started this book club. You can't help but care what happens to people you've known that long. Have I said this before?

Val was leaving—EOS. I'd miss her even though she has been at the governor's house for months and I had only seen her intermittently. I'd miss her knowledge of the system.

Pammie was also EOS, and she'd be out in another six months—and good for her, if she could keep her head down till then. And if she couldn't, nobody could.

Keisha—even Keisha had left—gone to Birmingham—and she was the one who said she would never go to Birmingham again. However, as a parting gesture, she did leave her poetry choices with Linda. Typical Keisha, organized to the very last parting.

We were down to four of our original members—five if you count me.

Of course, we had newbies to take their places but . . . newbies are newbies.

Ms. Foley, Linda, Uma, Pammie, and four newbies.

And evidently, we had added not one but two guests this time.

The first one was a Martha Castleman—a friend and across-the-aisle bunkmate of Uma's. With prompting from Uma, she began to tell her story.

We all settled back, enjoying our refreshments and listening. It seems Martha had married a man who abused her, and after a while she was accused of killing him, but according to Martha, the system framed her. She had had a baby when she was fifteen and another child, a boy, by the abuser a few years later. The whole thing was not her fault.

I have heard this same story in so many ways over the years in book club. Why don't these women ever just walk away? Easy for me to say. I think it must be a generational thing—passed down from one generation to the next—the mother who gets pregnant—doesn't love the child so the child is needy and then the child goes out and gets pregnant early—also looking for the love she never had . . . on and on.

But then again, I have to keep reminding myself, what do I know? Each month, coming here, it's like visiting another country. I am so ordinarily middle class. I've only gotten two parking tickets in my entire life—don't laugh. All us people who abide by the law, work regular jobs, love our children, stop at stop signs, go vote, and pick up the trash on the side of the road—we are boring, ordinary, dull, dreary—the bedrock.

Our other guest was Flora Lee. I was afraid that Flora might be a little high to begin with because she was so restless and fidgeting in her chair while listening to Martha, but it turned out that was just Flora Lee's way. She's a friend of Ms. Foley's and Ms. Foley does not associate with druggies—well, she might make an exception for reformed druggies.

Ms. Foley winked at me. "You gonna like her. She's been in and out of here forever."

"Is that right?"

"Yeah, and her sister is in here too. Come back in again just last week."

"Family reunion—nice."

"I like her sister too, but she ain't that much of a talker as Flora Lee is."

"She's not going to talk the whole time, is she?" I whispered. "We have an interesting read this time, with our poem choices and all, and I want to get to it."

"I'll keep her short."

With that, Flora Lee took the floor.

"Well, now, the last time I was getting lonely and wanted to get back to it . . ."

I squinted, "Uh, back to what?"

"Back to here, of course." Flora Lee looked at me like I wasn't too bright.

"Oh . . . of course." I nodded.

Flora Lee forgave me and continued. "So, I'm tellin' y'all 'bout the last time I come back in. Course they has been others—hello—plenty of others, but this was the last time." She gave me a condescending glance and continued.

During the course of the telling, I would learn that Flora Lee was not the ordinary lifer. She wasn't even a lifer, as I had assumed when I was told she had been since 1980. She was a constant repeater and had been in and *out* of jail since 1980. Evidently by the telling of this story, she was trying to get back *in* jail.

She continued: "So there I was, hangin' at the Texaco station in downtown Luverne. The nights was gettin' cold and somewhere along the way I done lost my rainproof Atlanta Braves jacket. And the policeman comes up to me and he say, 'Gas station fellow in there, he says you been hangin' out all day and tried to lift some potato chips last time you come in his store. Says he's gettin' tired of havin' to watch out after you 'cause he can't get no work done'—He looks at me like I was no better'n dog doo and he takes out his pad and I am thinkin', it gonna be good sleepin' tonight."

"He say, 'What's your name, girlie?'

"I smile up at him, my most innocent smile. 'Officer, I say, my name is . . . Condoleezza Rice.'

"I'm thinkin' he'll bust me just for usin' her name—her bein' a good Alabama girl, born and bred here, but he don't have a clue. He pulls out his pencil and says, 'Okay, how do you spell that?'

"And I am thinkin', Hell, I'll never get back in with this bumpkin.

"So, I says, 'Well now, let me seeeee here. It's C, O, N,' . . . and I pause like I'm thinkin' hard. Finally, he gets it."

"'This here is your name and you don't even know how to spell it? Get in the patrol car, girlie, I'm taking you to the station.'

"I shake my head, moanin' like, 'Oh me, I'm done busted'—and all the time I'm thinkin', Hot damn, three hots and a cot tonight."

By this time, the rest of the book club is roaring with laughter, and so am I. You gotta give some points for creativity . . . don't ya?

After a while Flora Lee had talked herself out, and we had finished our food, so now we could get to our poetic choices. Our guests would sit politely and listen while we talked about our book of the month—*101 Great American Poems*.

I had been surprised by how much they liked it when I gave out the book on my last visit. The minute *101 Great American Poems* was in their hands, everyone began to leaf through their copy, not listening to a word I said about anything else.

Ms. Foley had begun reading as soon as I gave it to her. "I remember this here one—from when I was a girl."

At the end of our session when I was packing up to leave, Uma—copy held close to her chest—had come over to me and asked to keep her book permanently.

"Sure, you can."

I had asked that they read all the poems and then choose the one they felt most appropriate to their life, or one that they related to in some special way. In the end, most had chosen two poems each.

There were lots of duplicate choices but I don't think it was copycatting because "We Wear the Mask" speaks to everyone who has to put up a front, and of course in here, with the guards changing the ground rules every day and the wardens coming and going and your fellow bunkmates here one day and (short-termers especially) gone tomorrow . . .

And of course, "The Road Not Taken." That one was made for this group.

Here were their choices:

Ms. Foley—"We Wear the Mask" (Paul Laurence Dunbar)

Linda—"We Wear the Mask" (Paul Laurence Dunbar) and "The Road Not Taken" (Robert Frost)

Uma—"Casey at the Bat" (Earnest Lawrence Thayer) and "I Sit and Look Out" (Walt Whitman)

Pammie—"Mother and Son" (Langston Hughes) and "This Is Just to Say" (William Carlos Williams)

Keisha—(who left her choices with Linda before she departed) "Mother to Son" (Langston Hughes) and "The Road Not Taken" (Robert Frost)

We had time for two readings. Ms. Foley volunteered to read "We Wear the Mask," and Linda, "The Road Not Taken."

Think of us, there in our little cubbyhole of a room, all pulled up around two card tables jammed together, the paper remnants of our refreshments scattered about the tables, the late afternoon sun finding its way in past the razor wire fencing just outside, and . . . we listened.

Here they are—to refresh your memory because, if you are like me, you haven't visited these classics in years.

We Wear the Mask
by Paul Laurence Dunbar

We wear the mask that grins and lies,
It hides our cheeks and shades our eyes,—
This debt we pay to human guile;
With torn and bleeding hearts we smile
And mouth with myriad subtleties.

Why should the world be over-wise,
In counting all our tears and sighs?
Nay, let them only see us, while
We wear the mask.
We smile, but, O great Christ, our cries
To thee from tortured souls arise.
We sing but oh the clay is vile

Beneath our feet, and long the mile;
But let the world dream otherwise,
We wear the mask!

The Road Not Taken
by Robert Frost

Two roads diverged in a yellow wood,
And sorry I could not travel both
And be one traveler, long I stood
And looked down one as far as I could
To where it bent in the undergrowth;

Then took the other, as just as fair,
And having perhaps the better claim,
Because it was grassy and wanted wear;
Though as for that the passing there
Had worn them really about the same,

And both that morning equally lay
In leaves no step had trodden black.
Oh, I kept the first for another day!
Yet knowing how way leads on to way
I doubted if I should ever come back.

I shall be telling this with a sigh
Somewhere ages and ages hence:
Two roads diverged in a wood, and I—
I took the one less traveled by,
And that has made all the difference.

There was momentary silence as we faded back into our world—then slowly began packing up to leave.

✳

Of course, nowadays, no good visit goes unpunished, and as I was walking out, a guard pounced. Seems to be the usual procedure now with our new warden in charge. I can't get in and out without someone berating me about something. This time, it's the brownies.

I was getting ready to be escorted out by a guard, walking past the administration office, when a passing lieutenant spots my empty tin canister that had held the brownies. "Whatcha doin' with that?"

"It had brownies in it. They ate all of them at refreshment time."

"Don't you know somebody could lace them things with marijuana or anything else you might think about?"

"I've been bringing them for years. My sister made them. I don't think she would even know how to do that." I smile. "We are a simple folk—of a bygone generation. The most we ever did in our youth was rum and Coke . . . uh, Coca-Cola, that is."

The lieutenant missed the humor and only became more incensed. I was subjected to five minutes of ranting and told never to bring brownies back again. "Anybody, I mean anybody, could get ahold of them and put somethin' in 'em."

I stood staring at her, a blank expression on my face, waiting for her to finish. I'm getting really good at doing my blank expression routine.

What was the use in mentioning to her that the first guard who checked me in earlier in the day had said the brownies looked delicious and I had offered her one. She had gladly accepted—and enjoyed it. Said my sister was a good cook.

A few weeks later a note arrived from Pammie. Seems—according to her—half the prison is now on drugs. Surprise, surprise, getting rid of my brownies was not a cure-all.

Dear Ms. Pat,
I asked the girls if they had some names to give you to add to the book club and they don't have anybody in mind. It's very hard to find good clean women in here that is about the right thing. Prison isn't like it used to be and this is between me and you on

what I'm telling you. Over half of the prison is on drugs in here. My mother has been sick in the hospital again and is still not doing good and Ms. Pat, Im so worried and stressed out. I just won't stick my neck out and add a member and they don't do the right thing by you. Can't wait to see you and I got the stamps.

Thanks, Pammie

CHAPTER 22
Our Very Own In-House Beer

Another new search procedure, introduced by our new warden. I was asked to empty out all pockets—no jewelry—had to take off my watch and earrings and return them to the car (which I left on the outside of the car in a wheel well as I had already turned in my car keys so my car was locked). Then a guard took me in the restroom and searched me again to make sure I hadn't tried to bring something else back in when I had gone to my car to leave the stuff I couldn't bring in in the first place.

Next, each book was searched—each magazine was searched—each parcel of food—no more brownies, of course. This time it took me forty-five minutes just to get inside. I wanted to say—but I did not—"this is not Tutwiler, people. This is a work-release facility and contraband flows like water in here." I wanted to say—but I did not—"If this place would make just one set of rules and stick to it for a while, everyone would be better off. Each time a new person or persons takes charge, a new way of doing things is instituted—as if the newbie is saying, 'This time things will be different, no drugs, no contraband, no disobeying *my* rules.'"

And, when I finally did get in, she wasn't there. Ms. Foley was long gone to Birmingham. How strange not to see her there after all these years, and how weird to see the flowerbeds all along the sidewalks—scrawny and drawn—already looking as if they missed her. She'd said she would be gone one of these days, but still . . .

I stood there watching the sunny breeze speckle the flower beds and remembered back to one of our many walks out to the gate after book club. I had asked her why, when she was first arrested all those years ago, Why didn't you plead manslaughter instead of murder—or maybe not guilty for reason of mental defect, or some such? In addition, some time back, I had done what one of the girls had suggested and gone to the clerk of the court in the county where Ms. Foley was arrested. I'm no lawyer, but to plead guilty to murder when you were OD on Xanax the day you killed him and he had been beating you up for years—and you were trying to save your child from the same thing happening to her?

"Surely your lawyer . . ."

"He done told me to plead guilty—to take a plea bargain. Said I'd get off with good behavior, so I done what he said. Afterwards, I found out I wouldn't get no time off for good behavior, wouldn't get no reduced sentence, none of that."

"Couldn't you appeal . . . in some way?"

"Done tried to appeal one time long ago. Had a friend in here, when I first come—her bein' a person who knowed 'bout the law. She tried to help me appeal but the judge and whoever else was in on it, they done denied it. That lawyer man I had, wasn't no account."

I watched the sun pass behind some scattered clouds and momentarily darken the impatiens planted along her walk. If the system ever failed anyone, it seems to me, it was Ms. Foley.

※

Later, she had even written to us from Birmingham—Sara and me. She had always liked to paint and draw and now she didn't have her gardens so she was relegated to art on a canvas instead of in the dirt. Sara took to the web and looked up requirements for what was allowed to be mailed to that jail and sent her paints and brushes. Ms. Foley in turn sent us pictures she had done up in Birmingham. Later we found out that Ms. Foley's desperation to get transferred to Birmingham was egged on by her desire to get to her mother's funeral when she died. Seems she was on the verge of passing and Ms. Foley knew if she went to Birmingham she would perhaps get to go to the funeral—different policy up there? Who knows. As it turned out, she did make it up to Birmingham just as her mother, who must have been in her nineties, died, and Ms. Foley got to go to the visitation but could not stay for the funeral. Both Sara and I wrote her notes of condolence and received lovely notes back. Sara keeps in touch when she can.

※

As I was turning in my usual salad and fruit yogurt order at the truck stop, I had forgotten and bought an extra salad—I was so used to having Ms. Foley there. Immediately Linda spirited it away—after I had suggested we divide it. Now, of our original ten book club members, only Uma the all-knowing, Linda the Librarian, and Pammie, wiping down table number 3, are left. All the while the newbies come and go.

When we settled in, before we began to discuss the book of the month, I wanted to know what they thought of the new warden. "Have y'all noticed all the changes the new warden has implemented? Have they helped any?"

"Why yes," Uma shot back. "Things done changed. There's a new kinda marijuana in here now—called Loud and it's five to seven dollars a shot, dependin'."

"Oh, peachy."

In addition, I was informed that recently Uma had had a birthday and to celebrate, some friends had gotten together and made a batch of beer for her.

"How sweet." The sarcasm was showing, but I couldn't help it. "You need yeast and lots of sugar and other things for that, don't you? I know y'all are creative, but where . . ."

Uma: "The kitchen, Miss Pat—really."

I suppose somehow, they must spirit it out from under the cook's nose or maybe the cook gets a sampling for her trouble.

"Right. Of course," I mumbled as I got out my agenda for the day. "And would you mind giving me a rundown of your recipe just in case Budweiser might want to know?"

Uma—who else?—took the floor. "Fifty to two hundred packets of sugar."

"Two hundred packets? Where do you come by that many—steal them one by one off the dining tables?"

Uma: "Do you wanna know or are you gonna keep on interruptin'?"

"Sorry."

Uma: "You buy 'em at the canteen—they come a hundred to the box."

"Oh."

"Yeast, two tablespoons of dry yeast. Two packets of ketchup."

"Ketchup? Yuck."

"Pay attention, Miss Pat."

"Sorry."

"Two packets of Kool-Aid (one small, one large)—I like orange—use the flavor you like. Two oranges and peels. Two orange Gatorades—in the cans. Two orange Faygo drinks. Add a quarter cup of hot water to a gallon jug. Put in everything and let it sit for about ten days to two weeks. Check each day to burp out the gasses. And be sure to burp the container at regular times—and don't shake it or drop it or it'll explode."

Uma turned to the others. "Remember Octavia? She tried hidin' hers under them blankets that time and forgot to burp it, and it exploded—and what a mess."

Remembering, or perhaps trying to fit in, the newbies laughed raucously.

"I can only imagine," I said.

Some time later I gave a copy of the recipe to my brother-in-law, who is a retired gourmet chef. I asked him if that list of ingredients would make up into a drinkable beer. "Well, Pat, I suppose, yes, if you're that hard up for a drink."

Pammie had burst in the door in the middle of our beer talk as she had been working, temporarily, at Tutwiler and the van coming back was late. She was filling in over at Tutwiler for another worker who was on sick leave. She plopped down in a chair, threw her book on the table, and heaved a loud sigh, happy to vent—and sidetrack the conversation—by expounding on the happenings of her day.

She had had a terrible one, she said—had been strip-searched two times, evidently in search of contraband. She and a few others took a prison van to Tutwiler every day and had jobs over there, sewing and such, but of course that left them vulnerable to smuggling contraband—and for that you get your share of searches.

According to Pammie, that day, while on the job, the other prisoners had a work stoppage because they were mad about being strip-searched so much. The dogs and guards had come again to search and this made everyone so mad they stopped work and lined up against the wall for bathroom break—supposedly—so then the warden came in and threatened.

During all these goings-on, Pammie was admonished by the other inmates because she, and a few others, refused to take part in the work stop. Poor Pammie. She just wants to go along to get along without too much hassle so she can remain eligible for release, and that's hard around here. Damned if you do and damned if you don't. Pammie is trying to live in two different worlds with two different sets of rules and get along in both—and it ain't easy.

Anyway, on to my reason for coming. Time to start thinking about football season. Well, almost any time is time to think about football season in Alabama. It is our state pastime. And so for this month's read I had chosen *The Blind Side*, which they all seemed to love. Most had heard of the movie and in addition they are all big football fans—cheering for Alabama or Auburn. This was right up their alley.

Uma: "Shame the kid in the story didn't go to Alabama instead of Ole Miss."

Pammie: "Or Auburn. Don't forget Auburn."

Linda: "He went because his adopted mama had gone there and he was beholden, of course."

Uma: "When it comes to football, you don't be beholden to nobody. Need to get the best you can when you can—and Alabama be the best."

Pammie: "Coulda used him on the line at Auburn last year. What did the book say he weighed, when he was a sophomore in high school—three hundred pounds?"

Linda, thumbing through the book to find the right page: "No, no they put him on a cattle scale and . . ." She found the page. "It was—he weighed in at 344 pounds—and a sophomore? Can you beat that?"

Uma: "That's almost as much as what's her name—Big Bertha—the one stays at the end of your row, Linda." Uma turned to me. "Lower bunk, of course."

"Of course."

The talk meandered between Alabama and Auburn football and *The Blind Side* and by inference, I could tell that they all had read the book of the month and enjoyed it.

We began to pack up to leave, but not before we had a brief discussion about which and how many newbies we would limit our book club membership to, now that we suddenly had several openings. In times past, one or two would leave and we would fill their slots, or we had tried having a guest of the month, but that hadn't worked so well, as the guest tended to take up all the time telling about her plight. Now we have openings for as many as four or five new members. Of course, my input holds little water and so I just listen. My only prerequisite is that the new ones be long-timers. No sense getting to know the group and our book club ways and then being gone the next month. Also, I believe the long-timers get more out of a book club than those who are just treading water, waiting. Linda assured me they would be, although she said that the place was beginning to fill up again—almost up to three hundred—but mostly short-timers. Next time, the four of us would discuss how many new members to bring in.

Upon leaving, the guard harangued us again.

"Don't wanna see no salads without the top sealed up. People can put anything in them salads. You gotta watch it."

And over my shoulder as I left, I called back to the guard: "I will remind the workers at Burger Joe's to be careful."

All the while, as I was walking back to my car, I was thinking, Okay now, exactly how would that work if there were marijuana in the Burger Joe's salads? (My God, the guard has reduced me to trying to figure how something that is completely nonsensical could ever make sense.)

Suppose I picked salads up at Burger Joe's, one exit up from the prison exit, and I brought them directly to the prison. Well, let's see. Maybe the mafia—maybe the Redneck Mafia, the ones who are after Dora Van, one of our former book club guests—maybe they are hiding the marijuana underneath the lettuce leaves in the Burger Joe's salad or sprinkling it all over the salad—must have an undercover agent assembling salads in the kitchen at Burger Joe's—and sending it into the prison to be picked up by an undercover mafia person in the prison. And then they would sell the marijuana to—well, it's bound to be rather wet by then, from the damp lettuce leaves. Who would want it? Anyway, they would sell it to their fellow prisoners—if they could get to it before Ms. Foley or somebody else in our group had scarfed down the whole salad.

Yup, that's it—Redneck Mafia conniving.

Or, if the inmates really want to get a buzz on, why go to all that trouble? They can more easily go get some in-house homemade beer and drink that—or maybe some hand sanitizer punch. Oh no. Then you cut out the Redneck Mafia's profit.

I slammed the car door, put the Honda into gear, and shook my head to clear out the crazies before driving out the gate into the real world.

Ms. Foley's painting of her childhood home

CHAPTER 23

And Now—Banning Our
Book Club Books

The weather had turned much cooler and that made for a more sleepable dorm and a better lifestyle all the way around. When I had handed out this novel the month before, I had read the definition of *dystopian* to prepare them for its theme. Uma was immediately taken with the word and began using it with everything. "You a dystopian kinda person, Linda," or "This place is downright dopey dystopian in here."

A good omen.

This month, to my surprise, the guard didn't even check my stuff on the way in, and although I had printed out my permission slip, no one asked for it. And another surprise. Uma was allowed to come outside the fencing and help me load the cart. Uma must have pulled more strings. She seems to have a certain rapport with the guards—most are Black. Our club tends to be about half and half—although with members coming and going now, it's hard to put a permanent percentage on it.

As we pushed the cart into the administration building where we meet, the guard didn't bother with an escort. She glanced at Uma and watched us go.

Of course, I had heard rumors from time to time that Uma is a kingpin in the drug cartel in here. I had noticed that the other members—the supposed clean ones in our group—do like her, but they seem to steer clear of her except when interacting with the book club. Am I like everyone else in that I believe what I want to believe and because she is such a likable person, I disregard what I hear? In any event, this particular time, the usual routine seemed to go by the board. What happened to the checking of the books page by page, the thumbing through of the old magazines, the inspection of the Burger Joe's salads, the banishing of the brownies? Like Alice falling down the rabbit hole.

Here is the really strange thing—I can't get used to not seeing Ms. Foley with her cart. Her flowers, along the pathways, are looking more and more bedraggled.

We still hear from her, up in Birmingham. She has sent us—both Sara and me—letters telling us she is getting along but missing her gardening, as she has nothing much to do up there but paint. Evidently, she enjoys reproducing pictures of her childhood. Sara has sent her more art supplies, and in return, she has sent us several lovely paintings.

Linda was the first to arrive after Uma. I gave them greeting cards Sara had created for them, complete with stamps on the envelopes, and they were delighted, as it is the main method of communication with family and friends—especially if you don't have money in your account for other contact methods, like video calls. Whereas if you have cards *and postage,* you are good to go.

When I came in, I noticed that Uma had a bandage on her hand and I asked about it, knowing that everything about her person has a story connected to it and if it doesn't, she'll make one up.

"Well, it was like this, Miss Pat. Ya see, last week I was heatin' some water in a plastic bottle to put in my bed to keep it warm—makes a good hot water bottle and great nighttime sleepin'."

I was impressed. "Creative thinking, Uma."

"Yeah, it is, but I commenced watchin' somethin' on the TV and forgot about it and by the time I took it out of the microwave, it spewed all over me and the girl standin' next to me. The other girl got burned a little but she wasn't hurt. Me, I burned the shit outta my hand."

"Oh gosh, did you have to go to sick bay or whatever they call it in here?"

A grimace. "Course not, Miss Pat. Wasn't goin' to any nurse and get reported and get me in trouble. I got a friend had Band-Aids and I got some antiseptic lotion from another one and then to disguise it, I put a glove on over my hand."

"And that didn't get noticed—wearing a glove on one hand?"

"Sure it did. Guard come up to me and say, 'Whatcha doin' with that glove on your hand?' And I say, now get this Miss Pat. I say—bein' real serious—'It's my tribute to Michael Jackson.' And I walks off—and the guard, she nodded her head and she walks off—and that was the end of that."

Linda: "I was standing right there. The guard walked right off like it happens every day—a newbie."

Only Uma.

As we were pushing our tables together, I asked, "How are things? The guards didn't seem to be as picky this time."

Linda sighed. "Same old same old." She gave me the napkins to pass out. "Here's my typical day now. I get up in the a.m.—I never eat break-fast—4:30 is too early for me. I police my bed—do my state job, which is cleaning the telephone booths." She notices my scowl. "I told you before, I like it because I can be *alone* when I'm out there cleaning the booths. I can be out there by myself all alone and nobody bugs me."

"And then?"

"And then I knit or crochet for the rest of the day—or do whatever, take a walk around the track in the exercise yard when the weather permits." She changed the subject, obviously bored with the monotony of it. "How's Ms. Foley? We miss her."

It seems I had now become the rather convoluted line of communication between Ms. Foley and those left in here. I suppose that if you have seen someone every day for years and then suddenly, they aren't there . . . I told them what I knew, that she was doing fine and painting as a pastime. "Maybe," I said, as a whimsical afterthought, "maybe someday both of y'all will get let out at the same time."

"Yeah—right, Pat."

Pammie came straggling in late, as she was doing laundry and then had to run by the canteen while the line wasn't so long. She was carrying a bag of items she had preordered and eating a frozen Popsicle that had been on her list—'I can't keep it sitting around."

Some people come away from the canteen with large sacks or boxes full of foodstuffs they have ordered. If you have the money in your account, you can practically live off the canteen food. If you have the money.

We go over the names of prospective new members. Linda named a couple of people and Uma suggested one she thought would like to join. Pammie said she wasn't going to recommend anybody—too much responsibility. We—they—decided on four possible new members.

"Fine. I'll bring seven salads next time and we'll have a welcome party. I'll bring some cute napkins." Napkins were about the only show of individuality allowed now with the new administration. A paper napkin with a logo on it or some other decoration was prized and immediately tucked away in a pocket for future show.

On to the book of the month—*The Giver*. A story famous to high school and middle school children throughout the country, and I thought some might have read it—but no one had. I guess it was published after most of them were already incarcerated.

I also thought it would be interesting to see if they might equate the world of *The Giver* to their own circumstances. In the imagined world of *The Giver*, everything is taken care of for you. You have no choices to make. Most all decisions are made for you—a socialist euphoria.

I had asked that they underline any particular quote that was memorable to them in this story.

Linda flipped pages to find the part where the Giver said to the boy, "Honor. . . . I have great honor. So will you. But you will find that that is not the same as power."

"It's like in here," Linda said. "Honor doesn't go to the ones that have the power. The ones that have the power—most of the time they just wanna use it to be mean so they can be the big boss of everybody. They *ain't* honorable." (I wanted to say, but didn't, "Learn to live with it, Linda, because you will probably never get out of here.")

Uma began to read her choice: "Things could change. Things could be different. I don't know how, but there must be some way for things to be different. There could be colors." Uma finished and looked up.

"Is it like life in here?" I asked.

Uma was instantly insulted. "Please—course not, Miss Pat—plenty colorful in here. Why, just the other day, had a dust-up in here—took two guards to break it up. Peoples can get downright mean and no stoppin' 'em." She turned to the others, who nodded in agreement.

Pammie was finishing up her Popsicle and pointed the empty stick at Uma. "That new guard, one with the fancy braid, don't believe I seen her back since she got in the middle of that one—got her nose broke, probably."

The others smiled, remembering.

Uma pushed back her chair. "Look here, Miss Pat. Most peoples don't like it in here—bad food, leaking roofs, mean guards, all that stuff, but ya know, some peoples do like it in here, least ways rather be here than out there. I got two next to me"—she gestured to the imaginary bunks on either side of her—"one over there and one over on the other side of me, in a high bunk. They rather be in here. Keep comin' back all the time. Say in here they can get drugs like outside and besides you get your food and a place to stay—clean clothes. Ain't all bad in here."

"Yeah, but *you* had rather be out," I said.

"Sure, but I got family to go to. Lotta people ain't got that. Remember that guest we had, Flora Lee, and her sister?"

Then the talk began to meander off in other directions—who would rather be in or out, who deserved to be in or out—even if they didn't have family on the outside. Just because you didn't have family on the outside, that wasn't—that *shouldn't*—be a defining factor, on and on, wandering around in the concentric circles of prison life.

✳

I had a special read for next month and wanted to spend some time talking about the author because I thought they might see a great life lesson in her experience—Anne Perry. I had brought one of her first novels. She has written more than forty—and I wanted to give them one of her early endeavors.

Her life story is this. When Juliet Hulme was fifteen years old and living in New Zealand with her English parents, she and her best friend decided to kill her friend's mother. They did kill her, and Hulme ended up in a prison in New Zealand for five years. When she got out, she changed her name and began to write as Anne Perry. Years later these events in her early life formed the basis of a movie. At the time of the film's release, it was not generally known that the mystery writer Anne Perry was the grown-up Juliet Hulme, whose identity was made known some months after the film's release. Anne Perry has since become a world-famous mystery writer, with her works selling over ten million copies.

The girls listened with rapt attention as I read a page or two of her autobiography, which I had found online. It would be interesting to see their reaction to her writing.

The time was almost up and I had everyone sign a quick thank you note to one of the women who contributed magazines every month.

All in all a meandering meeting but a good one—however, nowadays no meeting gets off scot-free.

As we were leaving (other inmates had come in and said they needed to set up for a church meeting that was scheduled), the guard in the administration office looked out, saw us, sprang up, pushed her desk chair aside, and rushed to the door.

Pammie was carrying a bag of old magazines, and Linda had the box of used paperbacks I had brought that would end up in the library or in some of their personal under-bunk boxes—I thought.

"What's in the bag?" The guard glared at me.

"Old magazines that they can read. I bring them every month. I have permission." I tried to look innocent and accommodating.

"Can't have no magazines in here." Having made that summary judgment, she moved on to the box Linda was holding. "And what's in that there box?"

I sighed and went along with it. "They're supplemental reads—old paperbacks, for when they finish their regular read. Just pleasure reading.

Oh, and the books of the month. There are some of those in there." Linda and Pammie had dumped their books of the month in the box in order to be able to carry the whole thing to the library.

"You can't have no books."

I knew it might not do any good, but I gave it a shot. "But I have a permission slip." I unzipped my satchel and fumbled inside to find it and show it to her.

She took it and carefully perused it. "You can't have no permission slip from the warden's secretary. You got to have it from the warden herself."

"Well, why then, when I emailed in my request for this month, did the warden's secretary give me written permission—if she can't give me written permission?"

The guard did not like this question. She stared at me, shaking her head all the while, and then stepped back inside her office. We watched through the glass partition as she picked up the phone to call the warden—so she said. And miraculously the warden was on the phone in one second and we could hear the guard, speaking loudly into the phone, for our benefit: "Can they have magazines and books?" Evidently either the warden had been waiting for her to call or she has telepathy. In any event, the guard slammed down the phone, stalked back out, and said, "No. The warden said no." And she summarily took the box of books and the bag of magazines from Pammie and Linda and chucked the whole thing into my arms.

"But wait, some of the book of the month reads are in this box. Can't I take those out so they have a book of the month to read for next time?"

"I said, *no books*." The guard was almost smiling but trying to contain herself.

"But this is a book club. What do you think we do? We *read books*."

The guard was not interested in logic. She walked to the main door, opened it for me, and with a swing of her traffic cop arm pointed me out.

"It's a book club!" I wanted to yell back to her, but what good would it do and what harm might it do to my book club members if I raised a fuss? Or maybe I'm just a coward to begin with. In any event, I weaved out the door, overloaded with my satchel, a big box of books, and a plastic bag of magazines barely in hand.

At this point, you are probably saying to yourself, What's the use? I know the system is in desperate need of halfway decent personnel or, more importantly, personnel that will stay on and learn the ropes and provide consistent services, but by the same token, why won't they even let those of us who are trying to provide a service at least try to provide it? I am beginning to feel like I'm one of those with a burned brain, and it would be funny, if it weren't so sad.

The following letter from Linda et al. arrived a few days after I got home.

Dear Pat,

First I want to thank you for all you do for the book club.

I wanted you to know that the way you were treated at our last meeting was unacceptable to all of us. It really affected me to where I don't know if I want to stay in the book club. I can't take seeing or hearing you or anyone else being mistreated or bullied, plus that wasn't the first encounter you've had with her. I don't know what her problem is, but she doesn't treat any black women that comes in here that way.

If you get all the confusion straightened out and still want to come, let me know. I would understand and commend you if you choose not to come again, but I would miss you. If you don't get anything rectified, before our next meeting date, then I won't be there. We take that abuse daily but you don't deserve it.

Write and let me know your thoughts.

Linda

I tried to keep my return letter above the fray, knowing that at the end of the day, I could leave and go home.

Hiya Linda and gang,

Thanks so much for your letter, and your concern. I too was disgusted by the treatment meted out by the guard this last month—as in times past. It was undeserved, not to mention uninformed. Having said that, I think the worst thing I could do would be to react in a way that would validate her belligerent attitude—by not coming back. I plan to write and get permission for everything I bring in—again—from the warden—or her assistant—or whoever is in charge—if that is possible.

I'll keep y'all informed and hope to see you next month.

All the best,

Pat

And from Linda, weeks later:

Dear Pat,

Thank you for trying to extinguish my anger toward a bully. She was trying to intimidate with a form of her bullying ways.

If you can handle it then I will keep trying to contain my thoughts in the matter.

I wanted to tell you that Uma escaped our apprehension with her book. I have recently found a copy in the library, so we are trying to read it before the 2nd.

Uma and Pammie are reading it now. Also I wanted to let you know that —— is now in the other book club. Please take her off of our expected list and to add another long-timer, ——. Black female with a life sentence and she's from Tuskegee, Al. She's an avid reader and would participate in our discussions. Let me know your decisions on the list of prospects we've given you. Hope to see you March 2nd.

Linda

CHAPTER 24

The Final Folly

It had been a couple of months since my last run-in with the book-eating guard and things seemed to have cooled down. At least none of the guards had hassled me lately. I have to constantly remind myself that they, as individuals, are probably not to blame, for the most part. They come to work here, are given a minimal amount of training, and then are sent out into the fracas. At least that's what I tried to think.

I arrived looking forward to this meeting, refreshed, with a new outlook—and we were to have more new members this time. It's always interesting to hear their stories and how they might relate to the books we read.

Pulling into the parking lot I could see my gang waiting in the distance. I gave them a thumbs-up as I got out of my car, which was packed with books, magazines, and refreshments.

Into the guard shack to check in. I was almost through the process when a lieutenant happened to come in as I was handing over my license to the guard who usually takes it and then calls for book club over the intercom. There were two or three other guards in the office checking out for the day, but the check-in guard stopped what she was doing when this particular lieutenant showed up and evidently decided that she needed to take charge and perhaps show off in front of the other guards. She took my permission slip from the presiding guard. Maybe she thought I could be an object lesson as to how you treat an outsider coming in. "So, let's see here what you got in the way of a permission slip"—a slight smile.

I handed it over—a slight returning smile.

She took her time studying it. "Hmmm, looks to me like you hadn't got everything you need here."

I had thought I would probably get more hassle at some time, and so I had checked with another volunteer to make sure my wording was right. "What's wrong with it?"

"Well, let's see here now. Looks like you bringing in a lot of food."

"The permission slip says I can bring in refreshments—Burger Joe's salads. I've been bringing them every month for ages."

"Refreshments means little things, like candy and such."

"Salads are better for you than candy—nutritionally speaking."

She again studied the permission slip. "Drinks? What kinda drinks you bringin' in?"

I almost said, "Bud Light, they need a break from the homemade stuff," but instead, "Sprite. Three bottles of Sprite—sealed, not opened."

"Brownies? Didn't bring any of them brownies, did ya?"

I bit my tongue to keep from saying, "No brownies this time. My sister ran out of marijuana to mix in the batter. Besides, they can get a better quality of weed in here, so why bother?" But instead, "No brownies."

The lieutenant continued to study my permission slip—and finally found something. "This permission slip says you're coming on Thursday. Today is Friday."

I took the permission slip and studied it and noticed down in the corner where it said *Date*, it did say Friday, but it had Thursday's date.

Busted.

The lieutenant glanced up at the other guards with a slight raise of the eyebrow, as if to say, "Told ya so." The other guards seemed not one bit interested, grabbing their keys as they left.

In my determination to make it right, I had not noticed, and neither had the other volunteer who had gone over it with me, that I had inserted the wrong date. And sure enough, there it was. "But y'all know, everyone knows, that I've been coming on Friday—for years." I looked over to the check-in guard, who nodded her agreement.

"Sorry, wrong date." The lieutenant tried for a benevolent smile—loving every minute of her authority.

"Would you mind just checking with the warden—see what she says."

"Warden ain't here."

I wanted to say, "So what's new—the warden is never here. Each time I come, the warden doesn't seem to be on the premises and when you check with the warden's secretary, the answer is always that the warden's secretary can't make decisions like that—so what kind of a squirrelly organization is this?" But instead I said, "Would you mind emailing the warden?"

Lieutenant took the permission slip and left to go consult with the warden's secretary—talk about useless—and we then began the waiting period to see what the warden had to say—if, that is, they could get in touch with the warden.

In the meantime, I chatted with the guard who usually checks me in. She had been absent the last few times I had come and said she had a second job now, to make ends meet, so she had had to change around her schedule a bit.

After a while, the lieutenant came back into the guard house, shaking her head, barely able to suppress a grin. "Wrong date. Can't come in, warden says ya . . ."

"So you're telling me I am to take $54.38 worth of Burger Joe's salads and fruit parfaits, not to mention bottles of Sprite, and dump them."

"Yeah. Warden says ya can't come in."

"I can't even give them the food and books, without coming in myself?"

The lieutenant shakes her head, looking at the floor so I won't see her expression. "Naw, can't do it."

"And next month's read, that I have in the car? Just forget about that?"

"Yeah—warden says you can't—too bad." The lieutenant turns abruptly to leave. On to more important things, I suppose.

At this point all I could do was stand there and shake my head in wonder at a system that has come to this. I had been coming to this prison for over seven years by then and had watched its ups and downs—mostly downs.

Wardens come and wardens go—the captains and lieutenants come and go—the guards mostly go, and it appears to me that the only ones in here who really know the ropes are the inmates.

On this occasion, all I could do was take a deep breath—and give up.

There is no other court of appeal—no other authority that I could petition to save the day—this day anyway.

I walked out of the check-in hut and passed along the chain-link fencing headed back to my car that still held Burger Joe's salads, used paperbacks, and yogurt desserts—all the while raising a hand to my people standing in a huddle off at a distance, watching.

When I opened the car door, I remembered that the one guard who had been civil, even pleasant to me, was still sitting there on check-in duty. In fact, that guard had been perfectly fine with my permission slip before the lieutenant came in and decided to show off. I remembered that the guard had said on several occasions how delicious the salads looked. I opened the back hatch, lifted up my cooler top and got out a salad, walked back to the check-in office and offered it to her. She was delighted to accept. My finishing touch to the perfect absurdity of it.

I ended up giving the remaining salads, still packed in their original plastic containers, to my niece's child to share with her friends, who were, at the time, sophomores at Auburn. Like they were in need.

⁕

After that last run-in, I grumbled for days, so frustrated with a system that seems pointless and counterproductive. We are warehousing human beings who have broken the law, and we send them to jail and school them in the various other ways of breaking it. In addition, the authority figures that preside over them do nothing but skew the inmates' idea of what real justice means. We aren't teaching justice; we are reaffirming injustice with this gigantic mass of humanity that we are storing like cattle in a pen.

And we wonder at the high recidivism rate in this state—in this country?

A week after I got home, this letter arrived from the book club gang—a group with perhaps more empathy for their fellow man than their keepers.

Dear Pat,

I really hated the fact that they wouldn't let you in because of a typo. It broke all of our hearts. We were hoping that you would of found someone homeless to give all of that food to. I was looking forward to our meeting with the newbies and talking about Antonia. What a great read.

I don't have money on my phone—hence me writing.

Always,
Linda

With a letter like that I had to think about going back—okay, maybe one more time—have I said that before?

And so . . .

CHAPTER 25
We Begin Again

Another fruit basket turnover. Now, the new rules are no salads of any kind allowed as refreshments, no extra paperback books for leisure reading, no old magazines for perusing in their spare time. Only one book per person and as refreshments, only fun-size candy bars.

And so we begin again—the circle of life, in the slammer anyway.

Before we began our book of the month, I brought up another topic, knowing it would only take a minute or two . . . won't I ever learn?

How steeped are we all in our own little worlds? It had never occurred to me to go back to the very beginning of book reading, the very, very beginning.

As an interesting point of discussion, I had brought in eight copies of a list of the best one hundred books for everyone to look over and see what titles we might be interested in for the future. Of course, after seven-plus years, we had already read quite a few. This particular list (and I know there are hundreds of lists like this out there) was divided into three categories—children's, with eight titles, young adult, with twelve titles, and the rest of the one hundred in the general category of adult. I gave each person a copy and asked them to look it over and circle the ones they might be attracted to and we would discuss. I had thought there might be a few of the young adult titles they would be interested in, but mainly I knew their attention would focus on the remaining adult books that were listed.

After looking at the list for a few minutes, a shy hand inched up slowly—Marlene—a newbie. "I ain't ever read any of 'em. Children's ones neither. If I did, I don't remember."

Me: "Well, some are just picture books—you probably wouldn't be . . ."

"I got a grandbaby—done turned six months." Marlene's voice trailed off. "I might be interested—for him, don't ya know?" A shy smile. "Mama didn't get me but just a couple of books when I was comin' up."

Me: "Well, some on this list are board books. Not much to read, just to look at, so . . ." I could see that Marlene was embarrassed that she had mentioned it, so I tried to back up. "But, come to think of it, they are beautiful. I believe they are meant to, you know, engage the child with bright colors and . . ."

Linda joined in. "I've got grandchildren I'll never see, so maybe it'd be nice to look at what they read, ya know, if they do . . ." And the look of an idea crossed her face. "Maybe I could recommend to them, if I knew something . . ." She looked around at the others and her face flushed. "Okay, I know I won't make this next go-round . . . long-distance Grandma . . . But if I ever did see them . . ."

Others began to chime in, knowing what I did not know at the time, that Linda had applied once again for parole that they knew she would not get—once again.

Anna, another newbie: "I got a girl—my mama's raising her. She's five now. I might like to see them picture books."

Pammie: "I heard of *Charlotte's Web*—made a movie out of it, didn't they? I myself never saw it."

Newbie Anna: "Yeah, *Charlotte's Web*. I heard of that one too."

Uma: "Okay, okay, seems like we need to go back to the very beginning and read some of them. You can go on and bring a bunch next time, Miss Pat."

"Well, thank you, Uma. I'll do that." I nodded and looked out at them, lounging around the table—my weary, longtime fellow travelers—and I couldn't help but grin. "Two roads diverged in a wood, and I, I took the one more traveled by, and I shoulda taken the other one—mighta made all the difference—book-wise that is . . . but it's not too late. For the next two months, I'll bring in some children's books."

Uma: "I know, I know—you're soundin' like 'The Road Not Taken.'" She gave me a superior nod. "See, I remember some of this stuff, Miss Pat."

I placed my list of top one hundred books back in my folder. "You're always one step ahead of me, Uma. So okay, next time I'll bring copies of *Charlotte's Web* for each of you and we'll go from there. I'll bring some board books too, for us to look at, and maybe others that might interest y'all, and your children. Hey, I might even leave some of them with ya, so you can send them on to your children . . . if I can get away with it. Then we'll go back to our regular schedule."

Uma: "Now you're talkin'."

"Now, on to our book of the month. This one, I know y'all must have loved . . ."

The end . . . I thought.

But of course, in our book club, the end is never the end, and this time, to my astonishment, two weeks after that last session, a letter from Linda arrived in my mailbox. One that I never dreamed I would—could—have in hand.

After the shock wore off, I pulled out a large cardboard box to begin gathering up books—her diploma—for all those years of bookin'. Proof positive that underneath the crusted remains of a system caving in on itself, perhaps there is a light of hope, ever so slight, blinking off in the distance.

Dear Pat,

I made it — I made it — I made it. 😊 My release date will come in a week or two.

I received your letter and passed it around. I may not be here for our next meeting — Hoo-Ray! None of us can remember the date of our next meeting. I've had too much happening. Now I'm focused on how I'm going to do all the things I have to do. I'm coming out of here with nothing and will have restitutions & halfway house rent to pay. It's alot to think about. I've got your number and will call when I get settled.

I want you to write ~~~~~~~~~ back and tell her the next meeting date. She is who I choose for you to correspond with. If you can send her some stamps like you did for me.

When I'm able to get my own place, I would like a copy of each book we've ever read in Book Club. Pack me a box of what you still have. And I will want an autographed copy of each one of your books, so put those in the box too.

I'll be in touch soon — take care.

Linda's letter

Acknowledgments

My everlasting thanks to all the volunteers who contributed over the years.

Dadeville Library, Dadeville, Alabama—Friends of the Pickens County Library, North Georgia—Toco Hills Public Library, Decatur, Georgia—The Beauty Shop, Dadeville, Alabama—Library in the Bent Tree Community, North Georgia—United States Tennis Association, Southern Section. And our individual contributors.

Many thanks to Brownie Caldwell, who teaches at Dadeville High School and was kind enough to lend me her tennis court lining gizmo, on numerous occasions. And to Bill Ozaki, who helped by providing tennis equipment from the coffers of the U.S. Tennis Association Southern stores. Lee Leach, my neighbor who is a master gardener and had just the right gardening magazines to engage Ms. Foley's interest. My good friend and tennis partner Jean Duke. I would search her collection of books left over from her various book clubs and abscond with them when she wasn't looking. Many thanks to Betsy Keown for her stacks and stacks of old magazines, especially People. My sister Joanne Walker, for her old magazines and her famous brownies and for the many, many hours she spent transcribing our inmate autobiographies. And Marsey Devoto, my fabulous copy editor.

And, of course, my sister Sara Cunningham Lindkrantz. Right before I finished this manuscript, Sara passed away after nine long years of her struggle with cancer. She was an ongoing inspiration to us all and especially to our book club. One of the last things she said to me: "Tell the gang to remember me as loving them."

Partial List of Books Read

Below is a partial list of the books we have read over the years, that I must pack up and send to Linda . . .

Mao's Last Dancer
A Thousand Splendid Suns
The Guernsey Literary and Potato Peel Pie Society
The Giver
The Tender Bar
Night
All Over but the Shoutin'
She's Come Undone
Shell Seekers
Sarah's Key
Snow Falling on Cedars
In the Garden of Beasts
The Nazi Officer's Wife
Seabiscuit
Harry Potter series
The Poisonwood Bible
The White Tiger
Memoirs of a Geisha
Cutting for Stone
Life of Pi
Bel Canto
Middlesex
Personal History
An Hour Before Daylight
The Pilot's Wife
Lord of the Flies
You Changed My Life
Midnight in the Garden of Good and Evil
I Know Why the Caged Bird Sings
Unbroken

To Kill A Mockingbird
The Blind Side
When We Were Sisters
The No. 1 Ladies' Detective Agency
101 Great American Poems
The Road
The Call of the Wild and *White Fang*
I Am Malala
My Ántonia
Anne Perry novels
Leila Meacham novels
The 7 Habits of Highly Effective People
Angela's Ashes

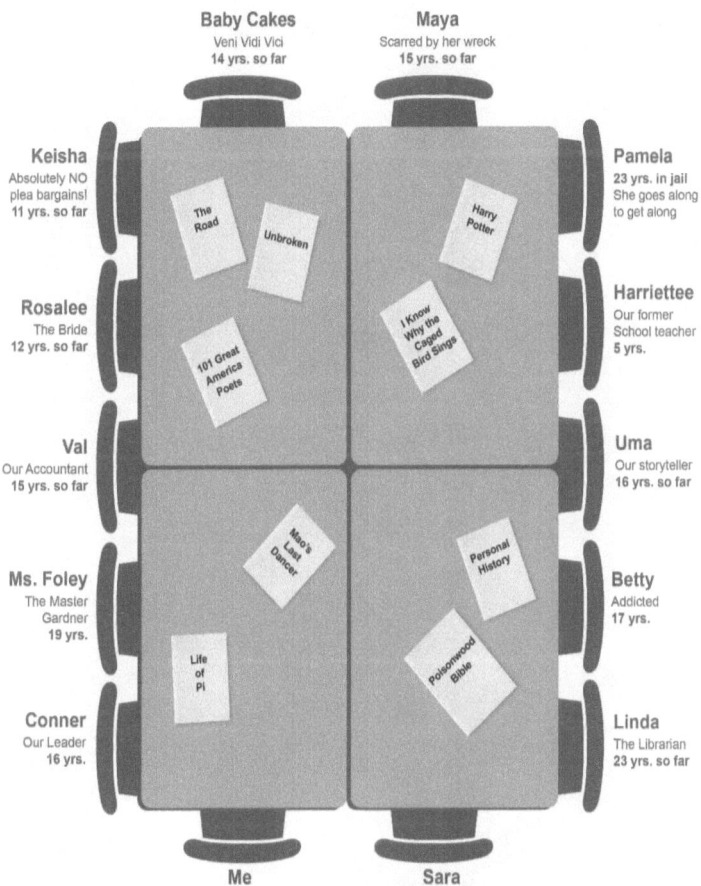

Baby Cakes
Veni Vidi Vici
14 yrs. so far

Maya
Scarred by her wreck
15 yrs. so far

Keisha
Absolutely NO
plea bargains!
11 yrs. so far

Pamela
23 yrs. in jail
She goes along
to get along

Rosalee
The Bride
12 yrs. so far

Harriettee
Our former
School teacher
5 yrs.

Val
Our Accountant
15 yrs. so far

Uma
Our storyteller
16 yrs. so far

Ms. Foley
The Master
Gardner
19 yrs.

Betty
Addicted
17 yrs.

Conner
Our Leader
16 yrs.

Linda
The Librarian
23 yrs. so far

The Road

Unbroken

Harry Potter

I Know Why the Caged Bird Sings

101 Great America Poets

Mao's Last Dancer

Personal History

Life of Pi

Poisonwood Bible

Me

Sara

Members of the book club, through the years, gathered around our book club tables